*New Directions
in Anglican Theology*

NEW DIRECTIONS IN ANGLICAN THEOLOGY

A Survey from Temple to Robinson

ROBERT J. PAGE

THE SEABURY PRESS · NEW YORK

ACKNOWLEDGMENTS

Grateful acknowledgment is made to the following publishers and authors for permission to use copyrighted material from the titles listed:

A. & C. Black, Ltd. (Dacre Press)—Kenneth Carey, ed., *The Historic Episcopate*.

Cambridge University Press—Alec R. Vidler, ed., *Soundings*.

Christian Century Foundation—Alan Paton, "Meditation, For a Young Boy Confirmed," *The Christian Century*, LXXI, 41 (Oct. 13, 1954), 1237-39. By permission of the author and of The Christian Century Foundation.

The Guardian—Monica Furlong, *The Guardian*, Jan. 11, 1963; May 2, 1963.

Harcourt, Brace & World—T. S. Eliot, "Burnt Norton," *Four Quartets*.

Lutterworth Press—E. R. Wickham, *Church and People in an Industrial City*.

The Westminster Press—Archibald M. Hunter, *Interpreting the New Testament 1900-1950*.

For Shary, Susan, and Sarah

Preface

I SINCERELY hope that this study will make a modest contribution to the sorely needed reform and renewal of the Church in this century. In human relationships, it is when one dares to be most fully oneself that one is able to enter deeply into meaningful and significant relationships with others. It is when Roman Catholics, Orthodox, Anglicans, and Protestants dare to be fully themselves that they find they have significant contributions to make to one another. To brethren of other traditions, I say, "Take what follows as a plea for, and an essay in, self-understanding. Be patient with us as we seek to clarify what it is that we truly are. In so doing, we hope to discover more of what it is that we may hope to share with you, even as we become more deeply aware of our deficiencies, which you, perhaps, may wish to help us overcome. The goal before us is that together we may witness to that fullness which belongs to Christ."

What originality this study may claim lies chiefly in the selection and organization of the material. I have sought to indicate my conscious debt to others in the notes which follow the text. It is also my hope that the notes may serve as a guide for those wishing to pursue certain problems which lack of time and space has made it impossible for me to treat fully in the text. I am keenly aware of the limitations of a study such as this. It is hazardous for an American to write about any facet of British life, let alone something as complex as the Church of England. For others it remains to write of the last twenty-five years with the detachment and perspective which will someday be possible. There is, nevertheless, some value in a preliminary report by an eyewitness and a participant. This is the reason for the present study.

Research for this study was carried out in part during the winter of 1962-63, while I was serving as visiting fellow at St. Augustine's College, Canterbury. I am grateful to the American Association of Theological Schools for a faculty fellowship which made the year in England possible, and to the fellows and priest-students at St. Augustine's College for many stimulating conversations and suggestions. My colleague the Reverend Richard M. Spielmann read three chapters of the manuscript, and the Reverend Richard F. Hettlinger read it in its entirety. To them and to The Seabury Press, I am indebted for many helpful suggestions. Mrs. Glenn Mayer typed the final draft of the manuscript. Without her patient good humor, a difficult task would have seemed insurmountable.

Contents

New Directions
in Anglican Theology

Introduction

THE outbreak of World War II coincided roughly with the
end of an era in Anglican thought. The period had opened
with the publication of *Lux Mundi* (1889), a volume of essays
by a group of Oxford scholars. The era as a whole was marked
by the philosophical background of British Idealism, the stimulus of historical and biblical criticism, a passion for social
justice stemming from F. D. Maurice, and the legacy of the
Catholic revival in the English Church associated with J. H.
Newman, E. B. Pusey, and their disciples. These elements
were found in varying proportions in the work of the chief
figures of the period. Their synthesis in the writings of Charles
Gore (1853-1932), and in a further composite volume, *Essays
Catholic and Critical* (1926), came to be known as Liberal
Catholicism, and was the dominant Anglican theology of the
period. This fifty-year span also saw the rise and decline of
English Modernism, represented by Hastings Rashdall, W. R.
Inge, and the journal *The Modern Churchman*. It was an era
that produced men of the stature of Gore, William Temple,
and a number of others only slightly less distinguished. There
was, in short, a genuine flowering of a distinctive Anglican
theology, comparable in some respects to that produced by the
seventeenth-century Anglican divines. The period coincided
with the zenith of the British Empire and its influence in Europe and overseas. It had about it an air of confident assurance
and a certain noblesse oblige.[1]

All this came to an end with the outbreak of the Second
World War. Its passing was noted by William Temple in a

I

prophetic article in the journal *Theology,* in November, 1939. Temple wrote of the gulf existing between his generation and the younger theologians whose work was beginning to attract attention.

There is a new task for theologians today. We cannot come to the men of today saying, "You will find that all your experience fits together in a harmonious system if you will only look at it in the illumination of the Gospel" . . . our task with the world is not to explain it but to convert it. Its need can be met, not by the discovery of its own immanent principle in signal manifestation through Jesus Christ, but only by the shattering impact upon its self-sufficiency and arrogance of the Son of God, crucified and risen and ascended, pouring forth that explosive and disruptive energy which is the Holy Ghost. He is the source of fellowship, and all true fellowship comes from Him. But in order to fashion true fellowship in such a world as this, and out of such men and women as we are, He must first break up these fellowships with which we have been deluding ourselves.

Temple stressed the need for a deeper awareness of the Church as a historic institution and the scandal of its divided state. He urged once again a renewed study of economics and politics in order to develop, in the light of Christian principles, "middle axioms," so that Christianity might play its proper role in shaping the postwar society.[2]

Returning to the task of doctrinal theology, he observed:

We must dig the foundations deeper than we did in the pre-war years, or in the inter-war years when we developed our post-war thoughts. And we must be content with less imposing structures. One day theology will take up again its larger and serener task, and offer to a new Christendom its Christian map of life, its Christocentric metaphysics. But that day can barely dawn while any who are now already concerned with theology are still alive.

The quest for unity among Christians, concern for a more just social order and deeper foundations for a doctrinal theology that would clearly proclaim to twentieth-century man his need and hope in a gospel of redemption—such was Temple's view of the dominant theological task in the postwar era. In the years that followed his death, his vision was imperfectly realized, and the road turned out to be very much more arduous and lengthy than he or those inspired by him could have realized in the trying years of World War II.

The break between the period 1889-1939 and the postwar years is not complete. Certain men such as Charles Raven, Leonard Hodgson, F. W. Dillistone, and W. Norman Pittenger seem clearly to represent continuity with the prewar period. For that very reason, perhaps, their work has not always received the attention it has deserved. Moreover, in the nineteen thirties, there were signs of a shifting of interest and focus, particularly among biblical and liturgical scholars. As Temple had foreseen, theology in the postwar years has been more humble and chastened in its mood as it turned anew to seek deeper foundation. The imposing speculative structures of the preceding period no longer carried conviction or even great interest.

The scope of the present study is the years 1939-64. It provides a convenient twenty-five-year period within which there is a certain unity. The contributions of Anglican theology have been modest, although not without their interest and importance. In the last several years, there have been signs of increasing ferment and, possibly, renewal bubbling to the surface. Such books as *Soundings* (1962), *Honest to God* (1963), and *Objections to Christian Belief* (1963) have deservedly found an audience outside Anglican circles. The situation out of which they arose and to which they seek to speak is of importance to anyone concerned with presenting the Christian message in the latter half of the twentieth century. There is, I believe, a recognizable body of Anglican thought which, in spite of many shortcomings, is of importance beyond any narrowly conceived ecclesiastical or theological boundaries. Moreover, in the literature of the last several years, one senses an important turning to fresh problems and questions that marks a new direction and vitality for Anglican thought.

It was possible to write of the period 1889-1939 in terms of several dominant figures. This is not the case for the postwar years. There is no one of the stature of Gore or Temple. It has seemed wisest to deal with broad currents of thought, by no means confined to Anglicanism, which have occupied the best minds of the Church, noting the contributions of various men to each of several areas of concern. The study is not confined to doctrinal theology per se. As we shall see, there is a certain occasional character about Anglican thought. It is at its best in dealing with concrete problems which arise in the everyday life of the Church. It has an innate suspicion of lengthy or elaborate theological treatises. In any event, with the possible exception of E. L. Mascall, Austin Farrer, and one or two others, the postwar years have not produced notable work in doctrinal theology from Anglican writers. If theology is the attempt to think coherently and reasonably about the meaning of the ongoing faith and life of the Church, the theologian must keep his attention fixed on those concerns that are uppermost in the Church's life in any given period. This study is essentially one in historical rather than systematic theology.

A. M. Ramsey, in concluding his survey of the theology of 1889-1939, expressed his conviction that, because of its insistence upon doing justice to the complementary and sometimes conflicting claims of scripture, tradition, and right reason, Anglican theology would continue to have a distinctive place and a contribution to make to theological discussion. A distinguished Anglican of a generation ago, Charles Gore, described his vision of the vocation of the English Church in these terms:

I believe with a conviction the strength of which I could hardly express, that it is the vocation of the English Church to realize and to offer to mankind a Catholicism which is scriptural, and represents the whole of Scripture; which is historical, and can know itself free in the face of historical and critical science; which is rational and constitutional in its claims of authority, free at once from lawlessness and imperialism.[3]

It is because I share the vision of Gore and the conviction of Ramsey that the development of Anglican thought is for me a subject of absorbing interest. There continues to be a vocation for Anglican theology which it has hardly yet realized.

William Temple spoke of the ecumenical movement as "the great new fact of our era." Its impact is being increasingly felt, not least in Roman Catholic circles. Is not Anglican self-consciousness, of which this book might be taken as an example, but another expression of self-preoccupation, denominationalism, or confessionalism, alien to what is clearly an ecumenical era? Let me state emphatically that I share Temple's conviction. It seems likely that future church historians will characterize the twentieth century as the century of ecumenism. Insofar as Christians may presume to speak of God's action in the troubled events of our time, it seems clear that Christians are being called to explore any and all means by which they may enter more deeply into unity with one another and thus serve more effectively that world for which Jesus Christ suffered and died so it might be reconciled to God, its Father and Creator. I wish to give no comfort to complacent denominationalism or confessionalism.

The Anglican Communion is that world-wide body of Christians, now more than forty million in number, which traces its historical ancestry through, and remains in communion with, the Church of England and its primate, the Archbishop of Canterbury. It is inconceivable to Anglicans that any "coming great Church" will be less fully catholic, less truly evangelical, and less genuinely open and sensitive to the world of men and ideas than the Anglican communion aims at being. No one knows its failures and shortcomings better than those who live and work within it. That reform and renewal on a scale scarcely yet envisioned by its most radical sons and daughters is required one cannot seriously doubt.

Consciousness of the Anglican Communion as a world-wide fellowship of Christians is a relatively recent phenomenon. The first Lambeth Conference, a consultation of those diocesan bishops in communion with the see of Canterbury, took place in 1867. The Anglican congresses held at Minneapolis in 1954 and at Toronto in 1963 marked the inclusion of priests and lay delegates at world-wide Anglican gatherings. Outside of Great Britain, the churches comprising the Anglican fellowship have been, and continue to be, preoccupied with the task of evangelism and the building of necessary facilities. The daughter and sister churches have naturally turned to England for intellectual leadership. In Britain, a long tradition of scholarship, the university faculties of divinity, cathedral canonries, a number of publishers interested in works of ecclesiastical and theological interest, and a comparatively compact literate audience combine to encourage continuing theological discussion. In the United States and Canada, there are signs of growing maturity and a lessening of dependence upon British intellectual leadership. Nevertheless, it remains the case that in speaking of Anglican thought, one means primarily Britain and, to a lesser extent, North America. One can no longer speak of Anglicanism without being aware of developments outside the British Isles. However, the major contributions to Anglican thought of the daughter churches in Africa, Asia, and South America still lie in the future. The concentration upon English writers in this study is intentional and reflects an actual situation, which, if slowly passing, was nonetheless a dominant factor in the last twenty-five years.

CHAPTER I

Thrust Toward a Critical Point

THE last several years have been marked by a growing ferment in Anglican thought, of which *Honest to God* is but one expression, albeit a particularly vigorous and popular one. The very fact of the ferment and the breadth of this literature of protest leads one to inquire about the soil out of which it has emerged. What can be said about the religious situation of the last quarter-century which helps account for the present climate of thought? As soon as one puts the question in that form, he is aware that the postwar years cannot be dealt with in isolation. The dominant forces which have affected Christian faith and practice since World War II have their roots in a more distant past. My intention is not to give an exhaustive account of religion in Great Britain in the last quarter-century. That task must await a more informed and dispassionate observer. Rather, I seek to comment on certain broad features of the landscape which serve to illuminate, and help account for, the swelling tide of ferment and protest. If the focus is primarily upon Britain, it is because the forces to be noted there are clearly present elsewhere in the world. As these forces become increasingly apparent elsewhere, the response to them in England will take on a heightened importance.

The Secular Challenge

In the present century, Christianity in Britain has found itself in an increasingly alien and uncongenial atmosphere. This is scarcely a new situation. L. E. Elliott-Binns observed of the nineteenth century that "the spirit of certitude which marked

7

the Victorians . . . did not extend to religion and philosophy." [1] Joseph Butler could describe the attitude of the world
of fashion of the eighteenth century in this manner: "It is
come, I know not how, to be taken for granted, by many persons, that Christianity is not so much as a subject for enquiry;
but that it is, now at length, discovered to be fictitious. And
accordingly they treat it as if, in the present age, this were
an agreed point among all persons of discernment; and nothing remained, but to set it up as a principal subject of mirth
and ridicule, as it were by way of reprisals, for its having so
long interrupted the pleasures of the world." [2] Butler was addressing a compact and highly literate audience who understood his exaggeration for the literary conceit that it was.

What is noteworthy about the present century is the breadth
and scale of the "retreat from Christianity." Christianity has
deep roots in England. For more than a thousand years, Christian faith has been an integral part of the life and culture of
the nation, combining fidelity to its past with a remarkable
capacity to adapt itself to changing cultural and historical
situations.[3] It is not possible to state with precision the point
at which Christian influences began to decay in England. The
tide of church attendance seems to have crested in the period
between 1880 and 1900. Thereafter, erosion of both church
attendance and influence clearly set in, and the rate of decline
steepened in the period between the two great wars. After
1940, church attendance increased slightly, but in 1963, the
situation, as described by Leslie Paul in a report to the
Church Assembly, was as follows:

In the country as a whole, though not everywhere to the same
degree, the Church of England is facing a loss of membership and
the attrition of its power and influence. It is not a new and surprising development, coming overnight, but the steady accumula-
tion of pressures and processes which are at least as old as the
century itself. In some cases they can be traced back to the
beginning of the industrial revolution; in others to the '80s, when

their peak and a recession began. Certainly they bear the mark of two world wars and a multitude of social changes. It might be wise to speak of the Church as being thrust by these developments towards a critical point rather than to use the overworked word, crisis, to describe what is happening, for the process is a slow one.

After listing a number of facts symptomatic of this "thrust . . . towards a critical point," Mr. Paul observed significantly,

But the massive shift of the Church from the centre to the periphery of affairs simply and perhaps properly reflects the shift which has taken place in the faith of ordinary men and women. The Church is not at the heart of *their* affairs as once it was, despite popular attachment to it as an historical and picturesque institution.[4]

The reasons for the "massive shift," of which Mr. Paul speaks, are varied and complex. A full discussion of them lies outside the scope of the present study. Some forty years ago, Charles Gore canvassed reasons for what he spoke of as "the breakdown of traditional belief." Chief among them he found to be the effects of Darwinism in popular thought; biblical criticism as it forced a new understanding of the inspiration and authority of the Bible; the comparative study of religions, which raised questions about the claim of Christianity to be *the* way of salvation for all mankind; and the revolt of conscience against certain popular forms of atonement theology which seemed to set God's justice in opposition to his love and mercy. Gore also took account of what he called individualism and "democracy" in thought, that is, the notion that everyone's opinion was of equal weight in religious questions, the rising tide of revolt against Christian moral standards, the effects of the widespread and needless suffering caused by World War I on belief in providence, and what he called "modern psychology." Gore concluded that a full scale "reconstruction of belief" was called for, and to that task he devoted the final years of his life.[5] More recently, J. V. Langmead Casserley has analyzed in greater depth what he calls the "retreat from Christianity" in the modern world. Professor Casserley speaks of two forms of the "retreat": into irreligion, that is, some form of rationalism, atheistic humanism, or scientism; and the retreat into religion, for example, natural religion, the cult of comparative religions, or one of the political religions of the present century, such as communism. He finds that the retreat into some other religion is the more characteristic form of the retreat from Christianity, and concludes by asking whether, in fact, twentieth-century man has advanced beyond Christianity morally, intellectually, or in social idealism.[6] Particularly valuable are Dr. Casserley's remarks about the sociology of the retreat, a line of investigation also developed brilliantly in E. R. Wickham's study of the relationship of Church and people in the city of Sheffield.[7] Wickham concludes that important as the intellectual difficulties facing Christians in the last century may be, the deepest roots of the defection from the Church as an institution are psychological and sociological. The basic factors which have shaped the modern world are the scientific revolution, which has made possible the technological and secular-minded society of our day, and the social revolution, which has thrown up a massive working class determined to gain its place in the sun and destined to make its own culture. The stronghold of Christianity in Britain traditionally had been among the middle and upper classes. The Church did not lose the working classes which emerged as a result of the Industrial Revolution. Numerous studies have made it clear that in Britain and elsewhere the churches never really had their allegiance. The greatest attrition of Christian allegiance and influence has taken place elsewhere. As early as 1909, C. F. G. Masterman could observe:

It is the middle class which is losing its religion; which is slowly or suddenly discovering that it no longer believes in the existence of the God of its fathers, or a life beyond the grave. . . . Among the Middle Classes—the centre and historical support of England's Protestant creed—the drift away is acknowledged by all to be conspicuous—by friend as well as by enemy. . . . It continues without violence, continuously, steadily, as a kind of impersonal motion of secular change. It is the passing of a whole civilization from the faith in which it was founded, and out of which it has been fashioned. . . . It is not becoming atheist. It is ceasing to believe, without being conscious of the process, until it suddenly wakes up to the fact that the process is complete. . . . The tide is ebbing within and without the churches. The drift is toward a non-dogmatic affirmation of general kindliness and good fellow-ship, with an emphasis rather on the service of men than on the fulfillment of the will of God. . . . The children are everywhere persuaded to attend the centres of religious teaching; everywhere, as they struggle to manhood and womanhood in a world of such doubtful certainties, they exhibit a large falling away. . . .[8]

What Masterman called attention to in the first decade of the century has continued and became increasingly obvious after World War II. The state of English Christianity at this time was aptly described, in another context, by Erich Meisner:

Religions . . . can go on existing after they have ceased to function. The doctrine is still taught and—so it seems—accepted; the rites, the customs, the ceremonies, the paraphernalia remain. There seems hardly any change at all, but the old words and terms sound hollow; dullness creeps in and takes away the lustre from the things that once stirred and invigorated the hearts of men.[9]

This judgment was corroborated by the report of a Mass Observation survey undertaken in Britain in 1947:

Religion . . . has in the minds of the great majority, become simply irrelevant to the question of living. It seems to have no connection with life and no relation to the real day-to-day problems of modern society. What has rightly been described as "a sort of inert agnosticism" seems to have settled on people's minds and the vitality of religious belief has quietly evaporated.[10]

Among those who continued to maintain an active Christian allegiance, the basic assumptions which molded their experience and behavior were increasingly secularist in orientation. E. R. Wickham argues persuasively that by World War II men's hopes everywhere were pinned to social engineering of some sort, that is, to a faith that the improvement of this life is by material means alone and that science and technology are the real meaning of providence for mankind.

However differently men construed the means to be employed, the ends to be realized, or the dangers to be avoided, these assumptions are axiomatic to modern man throughout the world, and as we have seen, they have a long history woven of the scientific and technological advance of the nineteenth century, and the growing selfconsciousness of the common peoples. The change that had come about in man's assumptions was so great that it is valid to speak of the emergence of a new type of man, with a new structure of thought and a new mode of apprehending reality.[11]

In sketching this aspect of the religious situation, it has seemed wise to quote extensively from native observers familiar with the English scene. In directing attention to an all-pervading secularism, there is no intention to minimize the moral, intellectual, historical, and psychological difficulties which affect faith in the modern world. These have been recently and ably canvassed by a number of books, of which *Objections to Christian Belief* is an excellent example. The sociological aspects of the situation, however, are less frequently noted by contemporary theologians and would-be apologists. Let us look at some of these.

The effects of industrialization and its attendant secularism are everywhere at work in the modern world. The problems raised for the churches by rapid social change, the break-up of older village culture patterns, the repeated displacement of masses of people in new and alien urban social settings, the psychological effects of the cornucopia of technology promising abundance and the satisfaction of man's every material need, the omnipresent welfare state offering a measure of security from the cradle to the grave, automation with its promise of greater leisure along with the threat of chronic unemployment, and behind this the all-pervasive secularism of the twentieth century—these are the massive and intractable problems which will be with the churches for a long time to come. The situation is much too complex to allow simple and facile "answers." In England, the situation is felt with an intensity not matched elsewhere in the English-speaking world because of certain features unique to the British scene. For centuries, it was possible to speak of England as a Christian nation; hence, the decay of Christian influence in recent decades is especially evident. The Church of England as an established church traditionally has felt a degree of responsibility for the moral and religious tone of the entire nation. Such responsibility cannot be assumed or felt by churches which are clearly only a tiny minority of the total population, which is the situation in Africa and Asia, or in a setting of religious pluralism which is characteristic of the American scene. The parochial system in England precludes the flight of churches from the inner city to the suburbs—one of the most depressing features of American church practice in recent decades. In England, a parish means a clearly defined geographical area, not simply a congregation of people which it so often means elsewhere. The vicar of a parish does not follow his congregation when they seek to escape the clutches of urban blight. They move to another parish, but their original parish and its vicar remain behind to face as best they can the attendant difficulties and evils of rapid social change.[12]

In Asia, Africa, and Latin America, along with the impact of Western technology, industrialization, and rapid social change, Christianity faces additional problems. Chief among them is nationalism. Those in the West who have experienced firsthand the fearful cost that nationalism has enacted in human lives and suffering in this century cannot regard its vigorous emergence in Africa and Asia as an unmixed blessing. But, of course, we speak as citizens of old, established, and victorious national states. To nations just coming to birth, both Western technology and nationalism are heady drinks. When the Church raises her voice in prophetic protest against injustice, whether in Johannesburg or Accra, she is treated in much the same manner as were prelates by Plantagenet or Tudor monarchs.

More often than not, the Christian Church is regarded abroad as the symbol and tool of a colonial era which has been swept away. No longer can the churches count on the novelty and once impressive character of Western ways to win adherents. The problem of the identification of the churches with European and American colonial and economic exploitation is a serious one. Moreover, there is now a strong resistance to any cultural imperialism, and the fervent desire to recover what remains of an indigenous heritage of art and culture. Inevitably, Christianity went to Africa and Asia clothed in Western cultural forms. Christianization often meant the destruction of older culture patterns and native artistic expressions. The resentment and resulting hostility is just now being expressed. Everywhere in Asia and Africa, new nations are saying to the West, "We are glad to accept your aid, your weapons, and your technology. We want no part of your religion and culture. We have had enough of that." Christian churches in Africa and Asia have scarcely begun to develop an indigenous art and architecture. In certain quarters, there is marked resistance to any such attempt among African and Asian Christians themselves. Some regard the imperative to do so as a tacit expression of continuing Western superiority: "You do not think we are good enough to make use of the best forms you have developed."

A significant feature of the religious climate is that certain of the ancient non-Christian religions, notably Islam and

Buddhism, are becoming missionary minded for the first time in centuries. Aware that Christianity has at best an indifferent record of success in checking the avarice and injustice which accompanies industrialization, educated Africans and Asians are taking a long look at Christianity's rivals among the religions of mankind. On a world-wide scale, Christianity finds itself in a situation of cultural and religious pluralism, more akin, perhaps, to the Hellenistic world at the beginning of the Christian era than to the apparently settled situation of the last few centuries, when it seemed possible for Western man largely to ignore other religions and cultures in the naïve assurance that he represented the apex of human development to date.

The task of the Christian Church is, as it has always been, to outthink, outlive, and, if need be, outdie its rivals. What is becoming abundantly clear is that both at home and abroad the churches are in a period of reappraisal in which many, if not most, of the older ways of commending Christian faith and practice no longer suffice. This awareness in many quarters helps account for the growing ferment among Anglican writers which is characteristic of the last several years.

The Church's Response

Faced by an increasingly alien and uncongenial atmosphere both at home and overseas, the response of the Church of England in the last quarter-century cannot be said to have been equal to the demands laid upon it. Broadly speaking, the period since 1939 has been one of transition, consolidation, and, to a certain extent, withdrawal. It requires an extraordinary amount of time, energy, and imagination, let alone material resources, to maintain the venerable parish churches and cathedrals of England and to put them to effective use in a rapidly changing world. That ever pressing task, together with agitation for revision of the Book of Common Prayer, studies looking toward the revision of canon law, the formation of new and independent provinces overseas in areas which had ceased to be a part of the empire, and concern for the training and deployment of the clergy, has absorbed most of the energy of the Church. Intellectual interest has centered broadly in three areas of concern: the ecumenical movement, liturgical renewal, and biblical theology. Such currents of thought are, of course, much wider in scope than the Church of England. In each of them, English scholars have made distinctive and significant contributions. Each of these movements offers promise of renewal for the Church, and must be among its continuing concerns. We will examine each subsequently as it bears on the vital question of the renewal of the Church in the present day. What is noteworthy, however, is that these broad movements of thought, together with necessary administrative matters which have almost totally absorbed the best minds of the Church, are matters primarily affecting the Church's own life. The world outside the Church has been almost entirely uninterested and unaffected. Meanwhile, the ruinous decline in church attendance and influence has continued. Moreover, this church activity, important and essential as it is, has been clergy centered and clergy dominated. Little headway has been made against the centuries-old tradition which makes laymen in the Church of England subordinate to the clergy in church affairs and, thus, effectively stifles serious lay initiative. "The Church which lives for itself dies by itself," Archbishop Ramsey had occasion to remind the delegates assembled in Toronto for the Anglican Congress in 1963.

The Church of England is an extraordinarily diverse institution. It is always possible to cite notable exceptions to nearly every general statement one seeks to make about its life and work. If the last quarter-century has been marked by a certain self-concern, consolidation, and withdrawal, one recalls that such periods are not uncommon or necessarily unhealthy in the life of an institution so long as they do not persist too long. The very success of the Church of England in times past left it ill-equipped to realize the full scope of the demands that an era of rapid intellectual and social change laid upon it. More-over, the picture of the last several decades is certainly not one of unmitigated failure. The period has had its prophets, among them Ambrose Reeves and Trevor Huddleston.[13] It has had a host of devoted and imaginative parish priests, of whom Er-nest Southcott, in his ministry at Halton, may serve as a symbol and example.[14] The construction of the great new cathedral at Coventry and the remarkably creative and outreaching pro-gram developed there by the cathedral staff is cause for rejoic-ing. The pioneering work of the industrial mission in Sheffield has inspired other dioceses to institute similar programs. In certain areas, the Church has shown great concern and imag-ination in its ministry to the vast new housing estates spring-ing up around the older cities and towns.[15] The various writings of Martin Thornton remind us of the vitality of the tradition of a disciplined spiritual life among at least a significant few within the Church.[16] The decline in ordinands appears to have been checked, at least temporarily. For the past decade, there has been a slow but steady rise in the number of Easter com-munions reported by the Church, although it remains the case that the rise is less than the rate of growth in population and remains only a fraction of the total number of those confirmed in the Church. Those attending public worship can no longer be said to do so in part out of the pressure of conformity to existing social patterns. The majority of persons no longer re-gard public worship as an essential part of the observance of Sunday. Those who attend the services of the Church do so because they consciously wish to be present. However encour-aging various developments here and there may be, the ob-servation made by Archbishop Ramsey in the midst of the *Honest to God* controversy remains valid: "Since the War our Church has been too inclined to be concerned with the organ-izing of its own life, perhaps assuming too easily that the faith may be taken for granted and needs only to be stated and commended. But we state and commend the faith only insofar as we go out and put ourselves with loving sympathy inside the doubts of the doubting, the questions of the questioners, the loneliness of those who have lost their way." [17]

In the United States, in the last decade, there has been a growing awareness of features of the religious situation common to Britain and the United States in spite of the many differences between the two countries. Samuel Wylie hails the passing of the white Anglo-Saxon Protestant "establishment" in the United States with a certain sense of relief and quiet assurance.[18] Perhaps no one has taken the "secular mind" of modern man with greater seriousness than Paul Van Buren. *The Secular Meaning of the Gospel* is a bold attempt to restate the essential New Testament message in thorough-going secular categories. If one concludes, as I do, that the result is a disastrously reduced form of Christianity, one must, nevertheless, pay tribute to the relevance and seriousness of Dr. Van Buren's attempt. Gibson Winter's *The Suburban Captivity of the Church* calls attention to the widespread flight of churches from the inner city and the resulting impoverishment of church life when its horizons are limited to a middle-class suburban enclave. *The New Creation as Metropolis* welcomes rather than views with alarm the vast urban complexes that are becoming the rule in the United States, and seriously wrestles with the mission of the churches to the entire urban complex.[19] The Detroit Industrial Mission, inspired in part by the Sheffield Industrial Mission, is carrying on an experimental ministry to the men engaged in the varied industries in Detroit. Basic research dealing with the attempt to come to grips with the realities of an industrial city and its accompanying secularism is recorded in *Christians in a Technological Era*.[20] *On the Battle Lines*[21] documents and records the growing awareness of the Episcopal Church of some of the dimensions of the situation it faces in the later half of the century as it seeks to exercise its responsibilities more fully. In Canada, such books as Pierre Berton's *The Comfortable Pew* and Ernest Harrison's

Let God Go Free are illustrative of a similar concern.[22]

One must hail with gratitude these signs of increasing realism and vitality in U.S. and Canadian churches. At the same time, it must be recorded that the forces with which the Church now shows increasing concern have been at work for many decades, and that the Episcopal Church has been even slower to recognize the changing climate, intellectual and social, in which it will henceforth exercise its ministry than has been the Church of England. It is high time we began to awaken out of our dogmatic and ecclesiastical slumbers.

The last several decades have not been ones of marked expansion and growth in the daughter churches of the Anglican Communion overseas. A number of new provinces have been formed, and ties with the mother church, whether in England or the United States, are much less constricting. With a measure of independence and its accompanying freedom, there are grounds for a sober and reasoned hope for the future in many quarters. What changes have been made are chiefly of an organizational and structural nature. One could scarcely describe the period as one in which the Church at home or overseas has been filled with a sense of mission and the spirit of evangelism. Nearly everywhere, there has been slow and steady growth, but everywhere the rate of growth in population has been even greater.

The problems faced by the daughter churches overseas are varied and complex. Always the opportunities far exceed available resources in terms of financial support and personnel.[23] In the United States, the journal *The Overseas Missionary Review* is a sign of growing concern in that most affluent of the churches of the Anglican Communion. Nevertheless, the degree of support for work outside the United States by the Episcopal Church continues shockingly low by any standards. Men such as Max Warren, John V. Taylor, and Stephen Bayne have written moving and trenchant accounts of the need and imperative for a deepened sense of mission. The program

"Mutual Responsibility and Interdependence," M.R.I., set forth at the Anglican Congress of Toronto in 1963 offers great promise.[24] It provides the opportunity for a renewed sense of purpose and mission which might revitalize the Anglican Communion both at home and overseas. The extent of its implementation over a significant period of time remains in doubt for the present.

In spite of an extensive amount of discussion and writing about the mission of the Church to "the world," and notable pioneering and experimental ministries, one who has followed developments in the last several decades may be pardoned a degree of skepticism. The renewed sense of mission, of which "Mutual Responsibility and Interdependence" is a symbol, has as yet kindled the imaginations of only a tiny minority within the Church, whether in Britain, the United States, or overseas. And even among those whose hearts and spirits have been warmed by the great vision it represents, one questions how many have really taken "the world" and its legitimate concerns with radical seriousness. There are all too many Christians whose concern with "the world" is essentially concern for a continuing source of raw material for the institutional church, not unlike the concern of the United States Steel Corporation for affairs in Bolivia, or the Standard Oil Company, New Jersey, for events in Libya or Saudi Arabia. The world of which many speak so glibly is God's world, which he has created and sustains in every facet of its being, that world for which Jesus Christ suffered and died that all men might be thereby reconciled to the Father, that world in which the Church and its members are called to live a life of joyous obedience and service to their fellow men, thereby showing forth their love and glory of the Father. When and if the institutional church sallies forth to be the servant church, "the world" may once more conclude that the Church bears some real resemblance to the Lord it professes to serve and whose "body" it claims to be.

The Theological Situation

In contrast to the fifty years preceding 1939, the last quarter-century has not been marked by outstanding theological work of a constructive and systematic character in Anglican circles. Good work there has been from time to time, notably by E. L. Mascall, Austin Farrer, Leonard Hodgson, and F. W. Dillistone in England. In the United States, W. Norman Pittenger has made significant contributions, and the work of younger men such as W. J. Wolf and Arthur Vogel leads one to hope for further achievements from them and their colleagues.[25] *The Canadian Journal of Theology* and a book like *The Church in the Sixties* are evidence of a growing vitality and independence in Canadian circles.[26] There have been outstanding historical studies of earlier divines such as F. D. Maurice, Gore, and Temple. Patristic studies have made real gains, of which the work of J. N. D. Kelly is representative. Over all, however, one cannot escape the impression that Anglican theology has been too much content to live off its own fat. What constructive work there has been is for the most part a continuation of traditions established in an earlier era. When one surveys the achievements of the last several decades as a whole, and compares them with the period 1889-1939, the contrast leaves one with little cause for optimism.

As we have seen, in 1939, William Temple anticipated that it would be some time to come before the sort of comprehensive and constructive restatement of Christian doctrine which he and his contemporaries essayed for their generation would again become possible. Such an enterprise depends to some extent upon a degree of unity in the fundamental assumptions an entire culture shares in common. The prevailing intellectual climate since the Second World War has been singularly lacking in any such common outlook, and pessimistic about the very possibility of achieving it. Earlier attempts at reconstruction were given to speaking with considerable confidence about the "assured results" of biblical and historical scholarship. But fur-

ther critical and historical research has repeatedly called into
question the "assured results" of previous scholars. Unsettlement both outside and inside the Church persists; and, in 1962,
Soundings opened with a statement that the time was still not
ripe for major works of theological reconstruction. "It is a
time for ploughing, not reaping . . . a time for making soundings, not charts or maps." [27]

Constructive theological work requires a firm and clear
grasp of the essentials one seeks to commend to others. Temple
had called for a proclamation of "the shattering impact upon
[the world's] self-sufficiency and arrogance of the Son of God,
crucified and risen and ascended, pouring forth that explosive
and disruptive energy which is the Holy Ghost." [28] It is precisely
that deep conviction and bold assurance which one largely
seeks in vain in the theological work of recent decades. Perhaps the very success of an earlier era of theology in one important facet of the theological task blinded theologians to
other still more basic undertakings and left the present generation of theologians somewhat handicapped in meeting the
challenge a later period made upon them. Noting that the main
occupation of Anglican theologians during the 1920's and
1930's had been, in the wide sense of the word, apologetic,
E. L. Mascall has written a trenchant warning to his contemporaries:

The movement had, however, its weaknesses. It was, on the
whole, too ready to accept the contemporary deliverances of the
secular sciences as reliable and ultimate; as a result of its natural
tendency to show how little a man needed to believe in order to be
justified in practising the Christian religion, it tended to a dogmatically attenuated type of religion which was somewhat lacking
in appeal to those who were not professional or amateur intellectuals; and . . . because of its anxiety to make Christianity ac-
ceptable to the modern mind, it was singularly impotent in
bringing a Christian judgment to bear upon the modern mind's
prejudices and assumptions in both the intellectual and social
realm.[29]

On the whole, a "dogmatically attenuated type of religion" and lack of prophecy have marked the postwar years without, however, the concern an earlier generation had shown in seeking to meet the modern mind on its own terms.

British theology has traditionally been somewhat isolated from, and uninterested in, developments in Continental and American theology. It is worthy of comment that A. M. Ramsey could write an able study of fifty years of Anglican theology without finding it necessary to make more than passing reference to anyone residing outside the provinces of Canterbury and York. This regrettable isolation of the English Church has persisted until very recently. Part of the shock produced by *Honest to God* was the lack of familiarity on the part of many within the Church of England with the German and American theologians whom Dr. Robinson quoted so extensively. In Protestant circles, the last four decades have been marked by the work of Karl Barth, Rudolf Bultmann, Paul Tillich, Dietrich Bonhoeffer, and of H. Richard and Reinhold Niebuhr. The writings of Kierkegaard have also been made available to English readers. One might have anticipated a revival of evangelical theology in some Anglican quarters, inspired and influenced by such Continental and American theologians. Both their style and message have proved largely uncongenial to Anglican minds, however. If read at all, such figures add at the most a provocative idea or two, a dash of spice, but have had little continuing influence. The same sort of observation can be made of Roman Catholic theologians and their influence. Men such as Yves Congar, Karl Rahner, and Hans Küng—whose theological work has both prepared the ground for and interpreted the *aggiornamento* symbolized by the Second Vatican Council—have been largely unknown in Anglican circles until recently; although there are now encouraging evidences of a growing dialogue on many levels.

An intellectual atmosphere uncongenial to major works of doctrinal theology, continuing isolation, and the awareness of the need for deeper foundations, biblical, patristic, and liturgical, have combined to encourage a natural tendency to turn to tasks other than doctrinal theology on the part of men who in another period might have devoted themselves to that central undertaking. Painful though it may seem, the indictment by E. R. Wickham of an earlier period very largely applies to the last several decades as well.

The supreme weakness then was a failure to understand the signs of the times, a failure of vision and perception, stemming from theological error that narrowed the claims of God and the concern of the Church from the dimensions of the Kingdom to the dimension of "religion." Inevitably it meant that the churches were preoccupied with their own affairs rather than the affairs of the world. . . . A failure of prophecy always spells a failure of sensitivity. There was the lack of creative tension with contemporary thought, and the strong emphasis on personal morality that either ruled out the issues of social morality altogether or restricted that concern to such social evils as patently issued in the most glaring personal vice. Albeit unconsciously, it was all calculated to produce a spirituality within the churches that was pathologically religious or highly conventional, lacking in understanding, sympathy and sensitive encounter with the estranged world. . . . The churches were good, but not good enough, penitent without understanding the complexity of sin, pious without a relevant spirituality, individualistic without being fully personalist, and corporate-minded without being sufficiently community-minded.[30]

What now seems to be taking place is a growing awareness on the part of many throughout the Church that the times call for renewal and reform on all sides if the Christian Church is not to be doomed to speak to a steadily decreasing minority in the modern world. In doctrinal theology, as in nearly every facet of its life and work, the Church is awakening to the fact that it is being "thrust toward a critical point." Certainly, an immense task of theological criticism and restatement remains to be undertaken. It will require the incorporation of material made available by the ecumenical, liturgical, and biblical movements, together with the psychological and sociological insights which are at long last being taken seriously by theology, at least in some quarters. The theological task is made difficult by the neglect of natural theology by all but a few, the narrowness of much theological work during the last several decades in Anglican circles, and the persistent preference of churches to become absorbed in schemes for administrative reform and mass programs to the neglect of doctrinal theology. Nevertheless, there are many hopeful signs that the somewhat pessimistic picture sketched in this chapter is giving way to change or at least to a call for change. To some of those developments, we now turn.

CHAPTER 2

Not Finality but Direction

IS THERE an Anglican theology? Apparently not. Writing about the Church of England in the century following the Reformation, Alan Richardson observed that an outstanding characteristic of the island church, in that century at least, was its abhorrence of insularity. "There were to be no distinctive English or 'Anglican' doctrines. The doctrine of the Church of England, so far as humanly possible, was to be that of every century and country." Dean Richardson went on to note: "This attitude remains the basic Anglican contribution to ecumenicity. The English Church was nothing other than 'God's Catholic Church' as it had manifested itself in a particular nation at a particular time; it was in the fine phrase of Bishop Cosin of Durham (1594-1672) 'Protestant and Reformed according to the Ancient Catholic Church.' " [1] There is, then, no Anglican theology in the sense of a distinct body of doctrinal teaching peculiar to the Church of England and its daughter and sister churches overseas. Stephen Neill has said, "In the strict sense of the term there is . . . no Anglican faith. But," he continues, "there is an Anglican attitude and an Anglican atmosphere." [2] It is this attitude or atmosphere, more easily experienced than analyzed, that gives to the work of Anglican theologians its distinctive stamp. It is this characteristic attitude—a method of approaching theological problems, the kinds of solutions that are felt to be adequate, a way of setting forth the Christian faith and commending it to the men and women of successive generations—that needs to be distinguished and commented upon. This chapter seeks to outline

certain continuing characteristics of Anglican theological writing.

Some Continuing Characteristics

An important feature of the Anglican atmosphere is a
strong sense of the importance of continuity with the historic
past and the heritage of an undivided Christendom. This finds
expression in many ways. In Great Britain, it is nourished by
venerable parish churches and cathedrals, most of which
count their past in terms of centuries rather than decades. A
significant proportion of them date from the Norman and
English Perpendicular periods, thus antedating the Reformation by many years. The Book of Common Prayer is a treasury
or anthology of the devotional heritage of the Christian
Church, incorporating as it does material from nearly every
period of Christian history except the most recent ones. This
atmosphere of antiquity is not simply a matter of beautiful
old buildings and an anthology of superb devotional literature,
however, nor is it confined to the English scene. Theodore
O. Wedel, for many years Warden of the College of Preachers
and Canon of the Washington Cathedral, writes movingly of
the Mennonite tradition in which he was reared as a youth
and then of his first experience of worship in the Episcopal
Church in a small Midwestern town in the United States:

. . . the worshipping membership was, somehow, not limited
to that gathered flock. Here was the Communion of Saints of the
ages at prayer. The prayers were themselves the "common"
prayer of uncounted Christians of the past, now mysteriously
joining with us in worship, though removed from our sight to the
Church Triumphant. The little Episcopal chapel, with its struggling
flock and underpaid minister, did not count very significantly in
the community. It was vastly overshadowed by the rival church
structures and congregations next door. But—and this is once
more the paradox of the Catholic heritage—I had the strangely
moving conviction that a majority was nevertheless in our humble
sanctuary.[3]

Regrettably, the majesty and beauty of its public worship can lead Anglicans to be complacent about the fact that their church frequently does not make a very significant impact in the larger community. Nevertheless, this sense of being one with the great Church across the centuries is not something to be scorned.

The importance of the heritage of the historic past is nurtured not only by architectural and liturgical forms but by the education an Anglican ordinand is likely to receive. The Church of England has valued a godly and learned ministry, and this tradition has, on the whole, been maintained both at home and overseas in spite of pressures to lower standards in order to secure clergy to man vacant parishes and initiate new work. The normal pattern is not to separate a man from the world and his peers until almost the end of his formal education. He is expected to live and learn side by side with men planning to enter medicine, law, teaching, or business, and to appropriate as much as possible of that heritage which belongs to all liberally educated men. Theological education and training follow in due course and are comparable in some respects to the specialized study of law or medicine. In spite of sporadic criticism that such a pattern of education is not producing men sufficiently well trained in mind and flexible in temperament to cope with the rapidly changing world in which they must minister, nor sufficiently expert in the practical aspects of the work of the ministry, the present pattern of preparation, with some modifications, seems likely to continue in the foreseeable future. For the most part, those most directly involved in theological education are convinced that the rapidly changing modern world places extraordinary demands upon education in every field. Gone are the days when a man might hope that the learning and techniques mastered in his professional training could equip him to meet the demands of his profession for the next forty years. The rate of change in the modern world is far too rapid for any such naïvité. Stress is properly laid, therefore, upon theological education rather than learning the practice of priestcraft. The way to achieve a greater professional expertise is likely to lie in programs of clinical training, internships, and residencies in specialized fields of work, and a greatly expanded program of postordination training comparable to what has become the rule in the field of medicine.[4]

The theology taught in the universities, theological colleges, and seminaries is predominantly historical in its orientation, rather than dogmatic and systematic. Whatever else a man may learn, he is required to master the Bible and the essentials of the Christian faith in their historical setting, and, hopefully, to come to understand their meaning against that historical background. If there is time, his teachers may make a few suggestive remarks about how the essentials of the Christian faith are relevant to, and might be commended to, twentieth-century man. Frequently, there does not seem to be time for this latter task, and the ordinand is left to work out such fundamental problems as best he can in his subsequent ministry. There is something to be said for this method as a whole, though not for its defects. Hopefully, an ordinand is delivered from excessive modernity with its changing fashions. He feels no need to change theologies as regularly as manufacturers change the design of automobiles. He sees that theology is firmly grounded in scripture and in a dynamic ongoing tradition of its interpretation by the Church, past and present. One ought not to be easily swept off his feet by the latest book or trend. More often than not, the perceptive man realizes that the latest fad in theology has much in common with earlier movements which have proved to be one-sided or misleading in one or more respects. There is a marked danger in the method as well—that of detachment, as well as the irrelevance of which theological professors are accused with monotonous regularity by their former students. Alec R. Vidler has written of the English scene:

Actually, our university faculties of theology, as at present constituted, would provide little or no scope for theologians qualified to show what their subject had to do with the problems and decisions that confront laymen in the public and private life of the work-a-day world. I do not know where theologians so qualified—for example Reinhold Niebuhr or Paul Tillich in the U.S.A. or the late Dietrich Bonhoeffer in Germany or that remarkable woman, Simone Weil—could be placed in an English university faculty of theology. Even if there were such places available, there are few, if any, English theologians who would be capable of occupying them.[5]

Dr. Vidler is perhaps too pessimistic in his analysis. In his own work and that of his colleagues, there is a marked awareness of the lack of relevance of much traditional theological study and writing, and a willingness to engage in dialogue with many aspects of the modern mind that has met with no little success. Nevertheless, one must grant his major contention. Traditionalism carries with it a certain aloofness, even distaste, for the concrete problems of the work-a-day world.

The effect of liturgical worship upon Anglican theology is difficult to assess. Certainly, it exercises a strong and all-pervasive influence. The regular round of daily matins and evensong in university, college, and seminary chapels, and the regular pattern of eucharistic worship in those chapels, cathedrals, and parish churches, exercise a steadying influence upon professor and prospective priest alike. Whether he is conscious of the fact or not, the words of the Bible and the Book of Common Prayer enter deeply into the mind and heart of both teacher and ordinand. They shape and color the ways in which a man experiences and interprets the activity of God in the world of today and in history. Moreover, the loftiest flights of imagination and speculation, and the most radical of lecture-hall theories, are refined, disciplined, and either assimilated or discarded in a setting in which the regular worship of God is an integral part of the daily discipline. The sources of theology in the Bible and the life of the worshiping community are daily brought home to the Anglican clergyman. Strange as the language of liturgical worship may be to minds shaped by our technological society, it is usually not so strange as the specialized language of the theological journal or lecture. The abstract and often obscure character of the latter is tempered by the regular use of the more concrete, imaginative, and dramatic language of the Bible and the common prayer of the Church throughout the centuries. The tension between two modes of discourse, neither of which is the language of everyday usage, is often felt as an intellectual problem of no little magnitude. How can one conscientiously use the language of the historic creeds or of a liturgy which constantly echoes the prescientific world picture of the Bible? It is all to the good that problems of this nature are an ever-present part of the experience of men preparing for the ordained ministry. They are certainly problems present in the minds of the worshiping congregations such men will someday serve.

A tradition which values highly continuity with the historic past is likely to have a certain distaste for novelty and extreme views of any sort. This certainly is a part of the Anglican atmosphere in general. A note on ceremonies at the end of the first Book of Common Prayer (1549) directs that "newfangleness is always to be eschewed." [6] At the end of the sixteenth century, one is not surprised to find Richard Hooker saying, "There are few things known to be good 'til such times as they grow to be ancient." [7] The Church of England has nourished children as bold, imaginative, and venturesome as any to be found in Christendom; but the predominant mood is cautious and conservative. The Church as a whole is not given to sensing quickly the signs of the times or to honoring her prophets in their lifetime, as disciples of John Wesley and F. D. Maurice had reason to learn to their sorrow. No small part of the resentment which books like *Honest to God* occasion in conservative quarters may be traced to this point. A bishop is not usually found lending his support to novel or extreme views of any sort. Conservatism and a preference for the tried and true are what one expects and finds expected of one in most circles.

If the theology of the Church of England ideally is that "of every century and country," one naturally would expect it to be unashamedly eclectic, and so indeed it is. There are no Anglican divines of the stature of Luther or Calvin. Although the Thirty-nine Articles may appear to be a doctrinal statement that provides the basis for a confessional theology, they are generally held to be a statement of the position of the Church of England in relation to particular doctrinal controversies of the sixteenth century. The Articles have nothing like the authority or influence that apparently similar confessional statements have had in other traditions.[8] At its best, Anglican theology ranges widely in its interests and in the sources to which it turns. It is as natural for R. C. Mortimer and E. L. Mascall to turn to the writings of St. Thomas Aquinas as it was for Hooker in an earlier era. The present Archbishop of Canterbury, Dr. Ramsey, has no hesitancy in acknowledging his debt to Karl Barth at a certain stage in his own development as a theologian, although Dr. Ramsey remains a staunch Catholic churchman.[9] Just as Anglican divines in previous ages quoted extensively from the early Fathers, as well as from St. Augustine, St. Thomas, Luther, or Calvin, so contemporary Anglicans refer to the writings of Paul Tillich, Dietrich Bonhoeffer, Yves Congar, or Henri de Lubac. Generally, it is to acknowledge their debt for a particular point or idea, never with any desire to associate themselves with the dogmatic system of another theologian in its entirety. There are those who deplore the fact that non-Anglican theology is almost invariably read in English translation, frequently only after it has been widely read and discussed elsewhere. It seems to be the case that Anglican theologians prefer their Roman Catholic or Continental Protestant theology in small doses these days, and often diluted by English translation. Most would plead with Hooker that "the law of common indulgence alloweth us to think [our own ways] at least half a thought better because they are our own." [10]

Fundamentals and Accessories

Outside observers are repeatedly baffled by the seeming neglect of theology, as they understand it, in Anglican quarters. There is a marked restraint, moderation, and even distaste for systematic or dogmatic theology as that task is usually understood in other traditions. This is no recent phenomenon due to the influence of liberalizing and antitheological forces in the last century or more. Anglicanism has a deep-seated suspicion of elaborate speculative systems of doctrinal theology. Consistently over the centuries and as a matter of principle, Anglicanism has aimed at simplicity and economy in its doctrinal requirements and expressions of belief. This drive toward an economy of essential doctrine is a second major characteristic of Anglican theological work.

In his controversy with the Puritans of the sixteenth century, Richard Hooker made an important distinction between *fundamentals* and *accessories:* between those matters "generally necessary to salvation" and matters convenient and useful in practice. Hooker held that the fundamentals were few and that they were revealed in the Bible and summarized in the historic creeds. The Church was not free to add to these essentials in its doctrinal requirements, nor could it dispense with them. The accessories were indeterminate and many. The Church from time to time properly determined and ordered those aspects of her teaching and practice which were accessories, guided by the light of reason and the direction of the Holy Spirit. The binding and loosing power granted by Jesus Christ to his Apostles and through them to the Church implied authority to decide disputed points of doctrine as required, and to decree and amend rites, ceremonies, and other matters of practice as time and circumstance demanded, so long as such decisions did not conflict with "God's Word written." [11] In the seventeenth century, the same note is struck by Jeremy Taylor, who insisted that men "should not make more necessities than God made, which indeed are not many," and by William Chillingworth (1602-44), who wrote, "I am fully assured that God does not and therefore that men ought not to require any more of a man than this, to believe Scripture to be God's Word, to endeavor to find the true sense of it and to live according to it." [12] The fundamental drive toward simplicity in doctrinal formulas is clearly expressed in several of the Thirty-nine Articles, and continues to find expression in the vow of the sufficiency of scripture made by each Anglican ordinand. [13]

This preference for an economy of essential doctrine is the basis for the Anglican rejection of the several dogmas promulgated by the Roman Catholic Church in the last century as dogmas based on tradition without being grounded in the Bible. It also accounts for the reticence with which Anglicans have viewed the speculative and rationalistic "systems" of many a Continental Protestant theologian. For the Anglican, the vitality of a theological tradition is to be found not in the extension of dogma and doctrine nor in the ability of a tradition to speak confidently on every point of perplexity which may arise. [14] Vitality is to be seen rather in fidelity to the apostolic faith recorded in the New Testament, which faith was further defined and defended against misinterpretation by the councils of the fourth and fifth centuries.

In the light of this background one can see that the insistence of the Lambeth Appeal of 1920 upon the historic creeds as a sufficient statement of essential doctrine has deep roots in the theological tradition of the Church of England. [15] That Church carries in its historical memory the scars of the bitter cost of doctrinal controversy over "accessories." In spite of the extraordinary skill of certain of its sons in the fine art of ecclesiastical diplomacy, it has not altogether succeeded in preventing schisms which have made it impossible for the Church of England to be the Church of the entire nation. The very diversity of thought and practice within the Church of England as it has come to be constituted has made economy of doctrinal formularies almost a necessity. The motives from the time of Hooker have been deeper than expediency, however, as the citations from the seventeenth-century divines above indicate. If, for the Anglican, the essentials of the Christian faith are summarized conveniently in the historic creeds, behind the creeds stands the Bible. The authority of the creeds rests not only on their well-nigh universal acceptance among Christians of all ages but upon the fact that they are a reliable summary of the self-disclosure of God recorded in scripture.[16] This helps account for the strong biblical and historical flavor of much Anglican theological writing.

The way in which these essentials of Christian faith, rooted in the Bible, summarized by the creeds, and defended by the great councils, are to be understood and commended to each succeeding generation is the proper task of doctrinal theology. Problems which in one age seem uppermost in men's minds may in a subsequent period recede in importance. Assumptions once widely held suddenly become problematic and uncertain. Analogies and arguments which once proved convincing cease to carry the weight that they previously bore. The very questions that men address to the Church—their deepest concerns and perplexities—change from age to age, and require a continual restatement of the Church's doctrine. Anglican theologians are likely to meet such demands by re-examining the nature of the essentials through careful biblical and historical study, and to write expositions and restatements of the faith of the creeds. Books of the latter sort are numerous, and some of them are very good, indeed.[17]

Authority and Freedom

Anglican theology is often described as a *via media,* or mediating, theology. The origins of this characteristic lie in part in the political necessities of the sixteenth and seventeenth centuries, when it seemed essential to seek a middle course between Rome and Geneva. As Hooker wryly observed, "Two things there are which greatly trouble these latter times: one, that the Church of Rome cannot, another, that the Church of Geneva will not, err." [18] Behind the political and ecclesiastical controversies there lay a profounder impulse, believes Paul Elmer More, "pointing in a positive direction, and aiming to introduce into religion and to base upon the 'light of reason' that love of balance, restraint, moderation and measure which . . . appears innate in the English temper." [19] Moreover, the student of the doctrinal controversies of the Early Church is likely to conclude that the true line of development lay not with the apparently simple, if extreme, emphases on, let us say, the humanity or the divine nature of Jesus Christ, but in their combination in a dynamic relation one with the other.[20]

The Anglican understanding of doctrinal authority in the Church cannot be simply stated. One facet of it is a deep distrust of absolute or infallible claims. In the seventeenth century, John Hales put the matter thus: "Infallibility either in judgment or interpretation, or whatsoever, is annext neither to the See of any Bishop, nor to the Councils, nor to the Church, nor to any created power whatsoever." [21] The crucial phrase is "created power." Both a sense of history in doctrinal controversy and a realistic appraisal of the human capacity to warp and distort the loftiest expressions of the human spirit is reflected here. Article XXI reads in part, "General Councils . . . (forasmuch as they be an assembly of men, whereof all be not governed with the Spirit and Word of God,) . . . may err, and sometimes have erred, even in things pertaining unto God." James A. Pike has recently written of the "churchmen's well-intentioned idolatry." "What is historically conditioned is presented as eternal, what is relative is presented as absolute, what is 'packaging' is presented as a product, . . . the notions of men are presented as the mind of God, the words of men are presented as the will of God." [22]

This innate suspicion of the authoritarian claims of any "created power" leads to a large measure of diversity of opinion and diffusion of doctrinal authority. Perhaps in no church in Christendom is there greater intellectual freedom. Probably nowhere is there a greater amount of clerical eccentricity as well. Anglican theology frequently presents a disorderly and chaotic appearance, not least in the present day. Writing of a comparable situation prevailing in the seventeenth century, Paul Elmer More goes on to speak of a "steady flow of the current beneath all surface eddies toward a definite goal." More observes that it was genius of Anglican divines in that period to avoid premature fixations of doctrine. He concludes that what one should seek from Anglican theology in any given period is "not finality but direction." [23] What matters are not the surface eddies, but the deeper currents beneath the surface. These are not easily discernible in periods of ferment, but they determine the future course that theology is likely to take. Because it clearly called for a new direction in theology, *Soundings* has been received with more than usual interest by those aware of this feature of Anglican thought.

At its best, the Anglican mind has sought to defend truth in the arena of free discussion, trusting the "light of reason" and the Holy Spirit to bring a deeper knowledge and understanding to men's minds. There are a number of polarities in the Anglican Communion: the traditional tension between those stressing the Evangelical and those stressing the Catholic aspects of its heritage and, more recently, the polarity between the traditionally conservative and the more liberal or modernist elements among Evangelicals and Catholics alike. J. K. Mozley noted a marked reduction of partisan feeling in the decades before World War II, and that tendency has continued, due in part to the unifying effect of the liturgical movement and biblical theology.[24] What is significant is that the Anglican tradition sees positive value in the preservation of apparently diverse points of view side by side. In honesty, one must say that the conflicting points of view are rarely brought into synthesis by a single theologian. Part of the greatness of F. D. Maurice and of William Temple lay in their capacities to do that better than most.[25] More often it happens that the diverse strains of thought seem to lie side by side, mutually informing those who come after. *Via media,* in a Maurice or a Temple, emphatically does not mean moderation in the pursuit of truth nor compromise for the sake of peace. And Charles Simeon rightly insisted that truth lies not in the middle, but in the extremes. It is the holding together of the extremes within one Church, while allowing them mutually to inform each other, that is the proper meaning of the *via media.*

The willingness to entrust the cause of truth to the arena of free discussion, and to allow diverse points of view to exist side by side within the Church, was put to a searching test when traditional interpretations of the inspiration and authority of the Bible and the literal interpretation of certain articles of the creeds were called into question as a result of biblical and historical criticism. Anglican theology rather hesitantly, and with considerable opposition in some quarters, decided the merits of the various issues in the give and take of open and free discussion. One result has been that the revelation of God is seen to lie not primarily in propositions to which the mind must give assent, important as these may be, but in the coincidence of divinely guided events and minds illuminated to perceive the religious significance of such events. "He guides the process; He guides the minds of men; the interaction of the process and the minds which are alike guided by Him is the essence of revelation," wrote Temple. "What is offered to man's apprehension in any specific Revelation is not truth concerning God but the living God Himself." Consequently, Temple argued, "there is no such thing as revealed truth. There are truths of revelation, that is to say, correct thinking concerning revelation; but they are not themselves directly revealed." These convictions led Temple to a functional view of the creeds and, indeed, of all doctrinal formulas.

. . . faith is not the holding of correct doctrines, but personal fellowship with the living God. Correct doctrine will both express this, assist it and issue from it; incorrect doctrine will misrepresent this and hinder or prevent it. Doctrine is of an importance too great to be exaggerated, but its place is secondary, not primary. I do not believe in any creed, but I use certain creeds to express, to conserve, and to deepen my belief in God.[26]

In summing up the discussion in England which extended over several decades and concerned the interpretation of the New Testament and the creeds, A. M. Ramsey has written, "There is less of a spirit of nervousness about the hesitancies on particular clauses of Churchmen whose adherence to the structure of orthodoxy as a whole is certain. A little untidiness is the price which the Church can bear to pay for its power to present the one Catholic faith with sensitiveness to the difficulties of an age. . . ." [27] Still more recently, Alec R. Vidler has written a brilliant "note" on authority and liberty in the Church; he concludes it by saying:

The greater the Church's trust in the absolute authority of God and in the promised guidance of the Holy Spirit, the greater will be its readiness to see its received doctrines and ordinances under constant re-examination. The Church has no doubt power to suppress or exclude those of its members who advance unacceptable opinions and may have on occasion to use it, but in view of the paramount importance of maintaining the utmost liberty of thought and experiment, and in view of the inveterate tendency of ecclesiastical as of other institutions to a blind conservatism, the Church should use this power with the utmost restraint. While there is a proper pastoral care in the Church to avoid scandalizing simple believers, there should be an equal care to avoid scandalizing the erudite and the educated.[28]

The Appeal to Experience

A further quality of Anglican theological work worthy of comment is what might be called empiricism. The word as I am using it has no direct connection with the honored tradition of empiricism in British philosophy, so far as I know, except insofar as the appeal to human experience for the data of both philosophical inquiry and theological reflection is natural to the British mind and temperament. Nor is there any conscious indebtedness to the theology of Friedrich Schleiermacher. By empiricism in Anglican theology, I have in mind the basic assumption that sound theological work is inseparable from matters of fact rooted in human experience. Consequently, one seeks to stick close to that experience, avoiding so far as possible a priori assumptions in approaching and understanding the data.

Near the end of his long life, Charles Gore sought to distinguish broadly between two methods followed in both philosophy and theology. The first he called the a priori method. Its outstanding feature is its "supreme confidence in the powers of abstract reason." In contrast, Gore himself was convinced that "distrust of the competence of abstract reason to decide what must have been or cannot have been, apart from faith, is a solidly grounded distrust which it is the glory of the physical and historical sciences to have wrought in the substance of the best modern minds." [29] Joseph Butler represented the contrasting method, which he, Gore, had made his own. Butler, too, sought a rational unity in all things.

He vindicates the doctrines of religion because of the identity of principle and method which he finds when he compares the doctrines of religion with the conclusions of natural experience. But he insists on sticking close to facts and experience. He disbelieves in the power of abstract reason, and in all a priori schematisms. He will not have the Word of God—that is God's self-disclosure to men—excluded a priori. It vindicates itself, he would show, by being close-knit into the fabric of natural experience which all admit. It is wanted to complete it.[30]

This is the method which Gore himself embraced. Sound theology draws its material from experience, and it turns to experience to verify its results.

"You content not yourselves with a moral certainty of the things you believe," complained William Chillingworth to his Roman Catholic opponents in the seventeenth century, "nor with such a degree of assurance of them as is sufficient to produce obedience to the conditions of the New Covenant, which is all that we require." [31] The note of moral certainty of which Chillingworth wrote, that is, a certainty sufficient for a man to act decisively and responsibly, is developed further by Butler and exemplified by Gore. It is a theme closely related to Butler's maxim, "Probability is the guide of life." What matters supremely is an assurance in moral and religious matters "sufficient to produce obedience to the conditions of the New Covenant." Here one feels that emphasis upon the moral significance and the moral consequences of faith that runs through British theology from the time of Pelagius onward. It may easily turn into an unlovely Pelagian moralism, pretentious of its own "virtue" and naïve about the depths of evil in the hearts of men. At its best, however, it is a theme congruous with the teaching of the Hebrew prophets and Jesus of Nazareth. It is an emphasis never far from an Anglican theologian's consciousness. Most recently the stress upon seeking the moral consequences of a belief or an experience purporting to be a revelation of God has been developed in a most suggestive way by Professor Ian Ramsey in his studies of the logic and meaning of religious language.[32]

The appeal to experience as the test for the validation of faith is a recurrent theme. Thus, N. P. Williams writes, "The final and clinching proof of Christian truth which raises 'probability' to certainty, for the intellectual and simple alike, lies in its verification through first-hand experience of God and of Christ in the Church and Sacraments." [33] Needless to say, the verification of which Williams spoke is a much broader principle than the verification principle of logical empiricism associated with the name of A. J. Ayer. The appeal is to human experience, but not merely to the evidences of the senses. Nor is it the experience of the individual alone, but the individual's experience as a member of a corporate body, the Church, and thus partaking of its common life and corporate rites. This communal experience is rooted in the past, in that experience recorded in the Bible and the ongoing historical tradition of the Church, while being at the same time a present reality.

In a theological context, then, empiricism means the avoidance of a priori categories so far as possible and the appeal to an experience which is both corporate and historical and, thus, never merely individual. It involves further the testing of a belief or practice, however venerable or appealing, in the light of its consequences, moral and practical. Verification of the Christian faith as a whole is inseparable from decision and commitment to the Christian life. Implicit in such an understanding is the willingness to examine one's basic beliefs and practices in the light of further experience, that is, openness to both reason and the Holy Spirit.

Anglican Flexibility

If the foregoing analysis is sound as a whole, it helps one understand the striking contrast between theological discussion as it is carried on in Roman Catholic or Continental Protestant circles and the bickerings among Anglicans over the adjuncts of worship and breaches of clerical taste. "That is the Englishman's way, to talk about what lies on the surface and to avoid as long as possible the deeper concerns of the heart." [34] The deeper problems emerge slowly, almost reluctantly, but they do emerge. Moreover, in the light of the foregoing discussion, it can be seen that a survey of Anglican thought cannot be limited to what is generally understood by dogmatic, or systematic, theology. The net must be cast wider to include thinking about the Bible, liturgy, the mission of the Church, its apologetic and evangelistic task, and its relation to the ecumenical movement. All these have been important in the corporate experience of the Church in the last quarter-century and, consequently, must occupy our attention. If Anglican theology has been less than successful in meeting the demands placed upon it by the rapidly changing world of the twentieth century, nonetheless, it has inherited from its past both a deep respect for the tradition of the elders and a high degree of freedom and flexibility to restate the traditional faith of the Church in an understandable manner and one appropriate to the changing thought forms of a new age. That is the significance of the historical survey undertaken in this chapter. Whether the resources of the past can be marshaled to meet the challenges of the present remains to be seen.

CHAPTER 3

Toward Deeper Foundations:
Biblical Theology

ONE of the more promising developments pointing toward a possible renewal of the Church in the latter half of the twentieth century has been the growing sense among Christian theologians of the religious and doctrinal importance of the Bible. This is not to suggest that the Bible has not been studied with great energy and application in nearly every period of Christian history. It is impossible to have a truly Christian theology which is not solidly grounded in scripture. Nevertheless, in the present century, it is chiefly in biblical and historical studies that the walls of isolation and sectarianism between various churches and their representative scholars have been broken down. There is a growing international community of biblical scholarship which cuts across established geographical and ecclesiastical boundaries. This community of scholarship and the cumulative results of its labors is one of the most powerful unifying forces in the Christian Church today. Moreover, interest in biblical studies has been shifting away from purely historical questions toward an emphasis on the religious and moral significance of the various sacred texts. Although I confine myself to discussing certain examples of biblical theology among Anglican writers, it is essential to remember that this is but one expression of a much wider movement. Within that larger movement, Anglican scholars have made and continue to make their contributions. Their work has no particular "Anglican" flavor, however, nor should one expect it.

44

The Critical Method

The application of the tools of literary and historical research to the study of the Bible is a relatively recent phenomenon. Significantly, this method, which is now called biblical criticism, has from the beginning been carried on chiefly by Christian scholars. It began in the German universities in the late eighteenth century and flowered in the century that followed. Newman, Pusey, and Samuel Taylor Coleridge were not unaware of the new method of study and some of its implications before 1850. Nevertheless, when Benjamin Jowett argued, in *Essays and Reviews* (1860), that "the Bible must be read as any other book," he was saying something generally new and startling in Anglican quarters. The inerrancy of the Bible had been a fundamental postulate of theological study for centuries. Thirty years later, Charles Gore's essay *Lux Mundi* (1889) noted that inerrancy was but one of several theories of the inspiration and authority of the Bible which had been held in the Early Church and then pleaded for acceptance of moderate critical results in Old Testament studies. This came as a profound shock to many of his contemporaries. The historical-critical method was firmly in the saddle in the British universities by this time, however, thanks to the scholarship of such men as J. B. Lightfoot, B. F. Westcott, and F. J. A. Hort.[1] By 1900, it was the rule in American Episcopal seminaries as well. Initially, the impact was felt most strongly in Old Testament studies, but by the first decades of the present century, the storm center had shifted to the New Testament.

The historical-critical method brought scientific methodology and objectivity to biblical studies. It had a fascination and beauty about it not always characteristic of theological study. The method seemed to hold promise that the origins of the Christian Church and the meaning of its sacred texts could at last be placed on a firm, objective, and scientifically

verifiable basis. Theological rationalizations and partisan ecclesiastical interpretations of crucial texts could at last be pared
away. The method aroused among scholars and students alike
the enthusiasm and high hopes that the application of scientific
methods arouses in any discipline when first put to use. If I
am critical of certain expressions of the historical-critical
method, I wish to be quite clear and explicit about its importance. It represents a gain in biblical studies of inestimable
value. It is impossible to foresee all the results that the method
will make available. Critical biblical study is a dynamic continuing process in which succeeding generations of scholars
check and, where necessary, correct the work of their predeces-
sors. There is a self-correcting factor implicit in the method itself. It is impossible for anyone wishing to live intellectually
in the twentieth century to seek to turn the clock back to a
precritical age as some conservative evangelicals seek to do.
One gladly acknowledges their fidelity to their Christian convictions, but at the same time must insist that they come to
grips with the method itself if they wish to be regarded as
serious and scholarly students of the Bible. The method is here
to stay. Let us rejoice in that fact. If the conclusions of certain
scholars appear destructive of faith, require modification, or
outright rejection, such results will be forced by an ever more
rigorous application of the critical method itself and not by
wistful appeals to the situation in a precritical age.

By the nineteen-twenties, in spite of notable achievements,
critical and historical biblical study had revealed certain serious difficulties. Literary criticism, the analysis of the various
sources and strata of material in the various books of the
Bible, had decisively undermined the older proof-text method
of appealing to an authoritative body of sacred writings.
Isolated texts, no matter how lengthy and imposing the list,
proved nothing unless and until one had examined the various
strata of material to which they belonged and sought their
meaning in the context in which they had been written. More-

over, analysis of various sources, sometimes carried to extreme lengths, was leading to a fragmented view of the Bible as a whole. All sense of the unity of the Bible and the development and coherence of its great themes of God, Man, Sin, and Redemption seemed to be slipping away. It was a positive gain to apply the tools of historical research to the Bible, to read it as any other collection of ancient texts. In so doing, however, the question of its inspiration and authority seemed to be shelved. The Bible was studied not as the record of God's self-disclosure to man, but as the primary source or sources for reconstructing the history of the origins of Christianity. This focus upon historical questions and upon matters of introduction, that is the date, authorship, historical setting, and intention of the various books of the Bible, so occupied scholars' attention that there was relatively less energy expended in the exposition of the meaning of the texts themselves. Questions of meaning and the contemporary significance of the biblical texts moved quietly to the background.

Still another difficulty became increasingly obvious. Although aiming at objectivity and impartiality, biblical scholars were unable, in fact, to approach the Bible without certain fundamental theological assumptions. These presuppositions, which were a dominant, if unconscious, factor in shaping the conclusions of many a Protestant and Anglican scholar alike, turned out to be those of that "liberal theology" which found its classic expression in Adolf Harnack's *What Is Christianity?* (1901). This theology was predominantly humanist and moralistic in its orientation. It emphasized divine immanence, the humanity of Jesus, the goodness of human nature, and the moral appeal of the Cross. The miraculous, eschatological, and transcendent dimensions of the New Testament were decidedly an embarrassment and tended to be rationalized or explained away, and all in the name of impartial scholarship. A wedge seemed to be driven between critical studies in the classroom or study and the requirements of the pulpit and pastoral ministry. The connection between critical biblical study and the Bible as that book which nourishes the religious life of Church and individual alike was in danger of being lost.[2] It is against this background that one must understand the reaction against "liberal theology" and its effects upon biblical studies which took place in the nineteen thirties and thereafter.

If the name of Karl Barth deserves only passing mention in the field of biblical studies, the beginning of a new direction and orientation was heralded by Barth's *Epistle to the Romans*. It was, in Barth's words, his "bombshell [thrown] into the playground of the theologians." "I wish," wrote Barth, "to understand and explain the Epistle, not to provide it with a series of illustrations. Paul knows of God what most of us do not know; and his epistle enables us to know what he knew." [3] Barth insisted that commentators have only done the work of introduction when they render Greek words into German or English and add notes of archaeological and philological interest. For Barth, exposition meant exposing the Word of God in the words of the text. However open to detailed criticism the book may be, and Barth has acknowledged that there is too much philosophy in it, the note struck was a prophetic one. The demand he made to see the Bible as the Word of God once more, to seek its meaning, to be humbled before its authority, was one that awakened a response in widely scattered circles. From this time on, one notes an increasing interest in questions of meaning as well as history. The unity of the Bible as well as its diversity comes to occupy the attention of scholars. A growing stream of books and monographs dealing with the theology of the Bible made their appearance.[4] In the period after World War II, the stream reached flood proportions.

In Anglican circles, the greatest single stimulus in biblical theology was the work of Sir Edwyn C. Hoskyns (1883-1937).[5] Hoskyns had studied in Berlin with Harnack, taking his degree in 1907. There, he had learned both a care for scholarly critical method and a passion for theology. From 1919 until his death in 1937, he was Fellow and Lecturer in Divinity at Corpus Christi College, Cambridge. His influence lay chiefly among his students, for he was not in any sense a popular theologian. In retrospect, two writings of Hoskyns's stand out as of particular importance: "The Christ of the Synoptic Gospels" in *Essays Catholic and Critical* (1926) and, with Noel Davey, *The Riddle of the New Testament* (1931). The former essay is important for several reasons. Its opening words make clear its main theme, namely, that there is the closest connection between the Christ of the Synoptic Gospels and the faith of the Catholic Church as it has developed in history. Hoskyns set forth the liberal Protestant portrait of Jesus, implying as it did a contrast between the Jesus of history and the Christ of Catholic faith. He then applied the tools of radical criticism to the portrait and demolished it on critical and scholarly grounds with no appeal to dogmatic theology or ecclesiastical authority. Having thus cleared the ground, he utilized the same critical tools for his own assessment of the evidence. As he does this, one sees emerging the Christ of Nicaea and Chalcedon, present in every stratum of the New Testament material. The essay does not allow a full summary because it is so compact and powerful. It must be read as a whole to feel its power and appreciate its depth.

The Riddle of the New Testament develops the fundamental theme which underlies all Hoskyns's work, namely, that there is the closest possible connection between history and theology in the New Testament. The riddle is a theological one because, insists Hoskyns, the New Testament is a theological book.

Study its text, analyse the Synoptic Gospels into sources, separate up the Gospel tradition into miracles, parables, and aphorisms [as the form critics were doing]—in short, push your way back as far as you can into the tradition, and you encounter Christology—you find, in the end, not a religious genius or the last and greatest Jewish prophet, whom the Primitive Church somehow transformed into a supernatural Christ, but One who saw in His own person and work the fulfillment of the Messianic promises made by God of old to Israel. . . . Properly interpreted by historical criticism, the New Testament documents converge on a single point—an act of the living God wrought out in the human flesh and blood of Jesus of Nazareth. In fine, the New Testament offers a concrete solution to the riddle of the world in terms of a unique Event—the coming of God's power and glory in the Life and Death and Resurrection of One who "according to the flesh" was a First Century Jew. It claims to provide in Jesus, the Messiah, the revelation which solves the deepest problems of human life, as it claims also that a decision by every man concerning this revelation is urgently important.[6]

Hoskyns died suddenly in 1937, with what was, perhaps, his greatest book, *The Fourth Gospel,* still incomplete. Nonetheless, the new direction in which he pointed was followed by his own students and by many others.

Creative Results

It is beyond the scope of this study to offer either a detailed account of the many facets of biblical study in the last several decades or to provide any full analysis of the various aspects of biblical theology.[7] Somewhat arbitrarily, several examples of creative work in this area by Anglican writers have been selected for comment—either as illustrative of certain tendencies of biblical theology generally or because the books or authors in question have sought and found an audience broader than that composed of specialists in the field of biblical studies.

A. G. Hebert first came to the attention of his contemporaries because of his translations, and, in the end, the word "translation" best describes his work as a whole. It was Fr. Hebert who, in the early thirties, introduced Scandinavian theology to the English-speaking world through successive translations of Y. Brillioth's *Eucharistic Faith and Practice,*

Gustav Aulen's *Christus Victor,* Anders Nygren's *Agape and Eros,* Part I, and Nathan Soderblom's *The Mystery of the Cross.* Others have since taken up the task of translating the work of these and other Scandinavian scholars. It was Fr. Hebert who perceived their significance and first introduced their work to an English audience.

It is for his work in biblical theology that Hebert is perhaps best known, however. Certainly, much of his energy lay in this area, as does the bulk of his published work. The most important books are *The Throne of David* (1941) and *The Authority of the Old Testament* (1947). Like Hoskyns, Hebert challenged the then dominant interests of biblical studies. He was critical of scholars for spending undue time on matters of text and introduction while failing to expound the theological meaning and significance of the books themselves. "All these questions which the 'critical' books raise are in truth only preliminary to the real study of the Bible, namely the study of what it was that the Biblical writers actually said, the study of the Bible from within." [8] It was the religion of the Old Testament and the theology which lay behind it to which Hebert directed his readers' attention. "That which makes the Bible intelligible as a whole is the conception which runs through it of a purpose of God in history. Perhaps this, more than anything else, can help the modern reader to see and love the Old Testament, if he can see that in the Bible something is happening, something which it is necessary for him as a Christian to know because it is essential to the understanding of his own Christian calling." [9] This vivid sense of God acting in historical events, disclosing himself and calling his people to repentance and obedience, finds repeated expression in Hebert's writings. A further note is his awareness of an underlying unity in the central themes which concerned the biblical writers. The books of the Old Testament were written by many hands over a period of centuries. There is frequently a marked diversity in viewpoint within particular books themselves that reflects the successive editorial revisions they had undergone. All the more remarkable is the underlying stress of the biblical writers upon the reality of God, the call of Israel to be his people, the stern demand for righteousness and justice, the repeated note of judgment, and the fruition of God's purpose for his people in the New Testament emphasis upon Christ and his Church.

Critical scholarship had rightly pointed out that the successive Hebrew prophets were primarily interested in matters of justice in their own day and not in predicting the course of future events except as they intensified the urgency of responsible moral decisions at the time. A consequence was that the messianic hope in its various Old Testament expressions receded into the background. Hebert asks whether there is not something important to be learned from the traditional interpretation of certain Old Testament "prophecies" as a foretelling of Christ. If the passages do not predict the coming of the Messiah in detail, nevertheless, Hebert argues, "Old Testament prophecies run to Christ as tidal rivers to the sea, only to feel his reflex influence upon them." The Christian Church as the New Israel, reconstituted with Christ as its head, is the inheritor of the promises made to Israel of old. Thus read, the Old Testament is sacred scripture for the Church. Its significance and authority are once more perceived.

One of the matters which troubled Hebert was that the new methods of biblical study had not proved to be the unifying factor that many had hoped they would be. In addition to the divisions created by centuries of schism within the Christian Church, there was also the division between those who accepted critical methods of biblical study and those who clung to a view of inerrancy and the plenary inspiration of the Bible. Hebert turned his attention to the position of the Conservative Evangelicals in his *Fundamentalism and the Church of God* (1957). To a considerable extent, Hebert felt sympathy with those who, perceiving the naturalist presuppositions of some criticism and its consequent lack of interest in theological questions, turned their backs on the method itself. But, argues Hebert, the alternative is a false one. The critical method has been used by successive generations of scholars who were and have remained believing Christians. The results of critical study are not necessarily destructive of faith; quite the contrary, the results of such study bring into focus the essentials of Christian faith and their close connection with the Bible as never before. Hebert then asks the Conservative Evangelical to consider how really biblical is the theology dear to his heart. Is it not unduly concerned with the individual and his personal experience of conversion? Does it provide a dynamic for corporate life and worship and for social action? Does it not make claims on behalf of the Bible and its writers that they themselves feel no need to make? A critical biblical theology is needed, not biblical theology without criticism. Those presently accepting the Conservative Evangelical position are urged by Hebert to join in that much-needed task.

If Hebert's work made too much of Old Testament events and archetypal figures which prefigured events and figures recorded in the Gospels, and if he was prone to read into certain passages meanings far removed from what their authors intended, nevertheless, his stress upon the Bible as recording the drama of man's redemption was a much-needed corrective to the one-sided emphasis upon source analysis and historical reconstructions. Hebert had a flair for asking the right questions and a flair for interpreting the work of others that helped to answer the questions. Theology chiefly engaged his attention, the theology of the Bible. He wrote primarily for the parish priest and preacher rather than for other scholars. Technical scholarship was not his forte. In his shorter books, particularly, he found a wide audience to which he interpreted the concerns of the biblical theologians.[10] He helped many to see the Bible and the study of it in an entirely new light.

Like so many of his contemporaries, Michael Ramsey, Archbishop of Canterbury, has made contributions in a number of areas. He is, perhaps, at his best in his balanced and judicious appraisals of the work of other Anglican theologians of the last one hundred years.[11] His essays in the field of biblical theology are worthy of comment, however. One is very much aware of the influence of Hoskyns. Thus, at the outset of *The Glory of God and the Transfiguration of Christ* (1949), he quotes his mentor, "Can we rescue a word, and discover a universe? Can we study a language, and awake to a truth? Can we bury ourselves in a lexicon, and arise in the presence of God?"[12] In examining the meaning of the word "glory" in both the Old and New Testaments, one finds that the linguistic study lays bare some of the greatest themes of Christian faith, among them Creation, the Incarnation, the Cross, the Spirit, the Church, and the World to come. The glory of the transcendent God is seen most clearly in and through Jesus Christ. His transfiguration anticipates and lends hope for the transfiguration of his Body, the Church.

The Resurrection of Christ (1946) combines careful, if sometimes conservative, use of historical criticism with a keen awareness that the Resurrection is the event from which both the gospel and theology have arisen. The treatment, therefore, is careful to survey the evidence for, and the meaning of, the Resurrection to the New Testament writers themselves, before turning to such questions as how it is to be understood in the present day and its implications for the Church and belief in the life to come. The chapters on history and belief and on history and criticism contain much that is valuable, not least their insistence that the New Testament yields its meaning only to those prepared to ask both historical and theological questions of it. The perceptive and appreciative references to B. F. Westcott and Henry Scott Holland serve to remind us that the sort of treatment demonstrated so ably by Dr. Ramsey is part of an ongoing tradition of theological interpretation.

A theology worthy of the name must be one rooted in the

Bible. Important as it is to come to grips with the modern mind and to seek to answer the questions it raises, the primary task in theological work, Dr. Ramsey maintains, is to do justice to the meaning of the great biblical themes and symbols. They are not to be explained away or trimmed to fit the presuppositions of a particular age. In the end, Dr. Ramsey is interested in theological questions: the authority of the Bible, the relation of the gospel to the Church, the great themes of glory and resurrection and their implications for the present life of the Church and its members.[13] His imagination is fired by the biblical symbols of flesh and blood, death and life, darkness and light, judgment and love. These are rooted in everyday human experience and, properly interpreted, are more readily understandable to modern man than the often abstruse language of would-be apologists.

"Professor Alan Richardson is a theologian 'whose praise in the gospel is (or deserves to be) in all the churches' on account both of the books which he has written himself and of those which he has edited," observed an editorial in the journal *Theology*.[14] One of the general editors of the Torch Bible Commentaries, Dr. Richardson has himself contributed two valuable books in that series. *A Theological Word Book of the Bible* (1950) has proved to be an invaluable tool for student and preacher alike. The succinct articles on the more important words and concepts of the Bible, some of the most important of which were contributed by the editor, both illustrate this type of biblical study and the extent to which work of this kind has occupied the attention of British scholars. It also demonstrates the ecumenical character of current biblical research.

Dr. Richardson's *Introduction to the Theology of the New Testament* (1958) is perhaps his most important book and represents a distillation of many years of research on the subject. Taken as a whole, it is an extraordinarily impressive and persuasive achievement. Here, one finds gathered together many recent developments in New Testament studies. The book is illustrative of the general climate of British work in the field during the forties and fifties and seeks to give a new impetus to the study of the theology of the New Testament. The major themes are examined with care, and there are abundant references designed to show the underlying unity of the themes. The thesis of the book, in Dr. Richardson's words, is "that Jesus himself is the author of the brilliant re-interpretation of the Old Testament scheme of salvation ('Old Testament theology') which is found in the New Testament, and that the events of the life, 'signs,' passion and resurrection of Jesus, as attested by the apostolic witness, can account for the 'data' of the New Testament better than any other hypothesis current to-day." [15] The tone is sober and judicious but rather more optimistic in its handling of the data than similar volumes written by Continental scholars. Dr. Richardson is aware of the temptation to impose upon the language of poetry and imagination an order and coherence which falsifies its import, but this does not dissuade him from his theme. Since its publication, the book has taken its place as the standard treament of the subject by an English writer.

Dr. Richardson has been very much concerned with the nature of the proper methodology for theological study and has recently written that "the development of an adequate methodology remains still the most pressing task confronting theologians in the twentieth century." [16] He dealt with the matter first in *Christian Apologetics* (1947). There is much that is valuable in this book, for example, the clear discussion of the meaning of the term "revelation" and the chapters on miracle and prophecy. There is a certain amount of special pleading, however, in Dr. Richardson's attempt to demonstrate that theology is one of the "sciences," and that its methods are as scientific as those pursued in other disciplines of scientific study. The definition or description of theological work is unduly narrow in that it seems to leave little room for a systematic and apologetic theology. Scientific theology turns out to be the biblical theology that Dr. Richardson himself expounds so ably. In his eagerness to maintain the independence and autonomy of theological research, he sometimes allows himself extreme statements, for example: "The only linguistic analysts of Christian 'religious statements' are the Old Testament scholars, or at least those who have listened carefully to what the Old Testament scholars say." [17] Very much more helpful is Dr. Richardson's account of the actual development of biblical studies which has accompanied and responded creatively to the scientific revolution. In *The Bible in the Age of Science* (1961), we are given a scholarly account of the development of the methods of theological and historical study in the last several centuries, together with many perceptive comments about the failures and shortcomings of those who pioneered in the new methods of research. It becomes clear that theology is closest to the work of historians, literary critics, and moralists. In any case, it is a broad discipline and nothing like as narrowly "scientific" as Dr. Richardson once suggested.

Limitations

Biblical theology as a whole is an enterprise which has engaged the attention of some of the best minds in all the churches. The movement has effected a recovery of a sense of unity of the Bible. The Bible is once again being seen as its own best commentary. If one is to understand it, he must enter as fully as possible into its characteristic modes of thought. Theological questions, questions of meaning, have been taken with renewed seriousness. The Bible is seen as fundamentally a theological book. Textual and linguistic study and matters of introduction are increasingly taken as prolegomena to the essential task of interpreting the meaning of the text itself. There has been a genuine recovery of the authority of the Bible as the Word of God, as sacred scripture, and not merely as a source book for historians. There is also far less willingness to interpret the Bible in the "spirit of the times" and to excise or explain away passages that challenge the dominant assumptions of a secular and technological age. An enormous task of recovery and reconstruction has been going on as the new methods of biblical study have rendered obsolete much of the work of biblical studies which antedates the use of the newer methods. This is an essential and continuing task which will be carried on by the Church and some of her ablest scholars.

Several decades of preoccupation with biblical theology have made many aware of some fundamental limitations in the movement. Biblical theology requires certain fundamental assumptions, for example, that the Bible is authoritative as scripture, as the Word of God; it assumes the actuality and authenticity of certain crucially important events in the past; it requires the proper interpretation of those events and a high degree of historical imagination and insight. Someone has dryly observed that "Englishmen (Americans, Africans, or Asians, for that matter) are extraordinarily uninterested in any history but their own." This may be a regrettable expression of human self-centeredness, but it is also the case in large measure. It is remarkably difficult for a modern man to grasp that the history of another nation and people, the ancient Jewish nation at that, can have a meaning crucially important for him today. This means that biblical theology is heard and heeded almost entirely by the faithful, the already convinced and converted. Its usefulness in addressing the "outsider" is severely limited. Biblical theologians themselves have been prone to indulge in isolationism, too often content to address one another while warning philosophers and systematic theologians not to poach in that territory marked out as their special preserve.[18] There are a number of basic questions, such as the authority and inspiration of the Bible, the meaning of miracle, providence and the fact of evil, and the nature and properties of religious language itself, which cannot be dealt with on any narrowly biblical basis alone.[19] Unless the prior questions which arise in men's minds are dealt with in some satisfactory manner, many—indeed most—outside the churches and not a few within them simply cannot hear what the biblical theologians are saying. It is urgent, therefore, that bridges be thrown across the chasm separating the "strange world of the Bible" and the perhaps equally strange world of modern Western secular civilization. Here, the biblical theologians as a whole have not so far provided very much help. Their former students are inclined to reproach them as being merely academic, when perhaps a more apt criticism would be that they have not been sufficiently biblical and theological.

The work of recovery and reconstruction in biblical studies can and must continue. It is precisely because biblical theology has in a sense turned in upon itself—become unduly specialized and esoteric, not sufficiently concerned to share its results with the Church and, beyond its bounds, with the world—that it is beginning to lose some of its power to kindle the imaginations of many of its admirers. If biblical theology answers some of our questions, it leaves many other urgent questions unanswered. It cannot command the enthusiasm it once did as providing *the* theology which the Church requires. Its tendencies toward isolation and subjectivity prevent this. Indeed, biblical theology itself demonstrates its need for renewed interest in precisely those questions of natural and doctrinal theology which it has neglected.

CHAPTER 4

The Promise of Liturgical Renewal

A SECOND major source of hope for the renewal of the churches in this century is what has come to be called the liturgical movement. If the following discussion confines itself to selected expressions of this concern in Anglican circles, it is important to bear in mind that these instances are representative of a movement very much broader than the Anglican Communion. Concern for the vitality and authenticity of corporate worship has powerfully affected the life of the Roman Catholic Church and, to a lesser extent, many a Protestant church as well.[1] Like biblical theology, it has proved to be a unifying factor within Anglicanism while at the same time revealing how much those deeply concerned with liturgical renewal in all churches have in common despite centuries of schism and diverse historical and ecclesiastical backgrounds.

We have already noted the subtle, all-pervasive influence of the Book of Common Prayer on Anglican thought and practice generally. Because of that heritage, one would expect that Anglicans would find the cause of liturgical renewal a subject of absorbing interest, and this indeed is the case. Of necessity, we must speak chiefly of the intellectual side of the movement, of certain influential figures, their books and ideas. It is important, however, to keep clearly in mind that the movement itself has its roots deep in the life of parish churches. If biblical theology has been largely the preserve of university and seminary professors, liturgical renewal has been a cause of absorbing interest to the parochial clergy. Without their efforts, it could amount to little. It is no accident, therefore,

60

that the groups most concerned, "Parish and People" in Britain and "Associated Parishes" in the United States, find it natural to use the word "parish" in their official titles.

The Background

What are the roots of concern for liturgical renewal in Anglican circles? A full account remains to be written.[2] The Oxford Movement stood for a renewed emphasis upon the Church and sacraments as divinely appointed means of grace. Thus, matters of liturgy, particularly the Holy Communion, were brought to the center of attention. Thanks to the Oxford reformers, there was a genuine revival of sacramental piety in the latter half of the nineteenth century that has continued down to the present day. If the movement failed to secure the Holy Communion as the norm for the chief service of worship each Sunday in parish churches, and this continues to be a major objective of liturgical reform, the prominence which eucharistic worship presently occupies throughout the Church is largely due to the influence of the Oxford Movement. Sunday celebrations at an early hour, weekday celebrations, and eucharistic worship on the major festival days of the liturgical year are no longer matters of partisan churchmanship.

In its later phases the Oxford, or Anglo-Catholic, Movement was frequently described as "ritualism," a misnomer since what was at stake was not primarily the words of the rite itself, but the ceremonial practices which accompanied it. Some of the ritualists were unduly concerned with the niceties of ecclesiastical millinery. One cannot account for the heated controversies during the latter part of the last century, however, unless it is seen that both sides recognized matters of ceremonial to be often expressive of deep religious conviction as well. Not merely appropriate behavior in church but an entire theological orientation was at stake. In their desire to enrich the public worship of the Church and to recover elements of its Catholic heritage that had been long neglected or fallen into disuse, the ritualists turned to earlier Anglican divines such as Lancelot Andrewes, William Laud, and John Cosin. Medieval service books were studied for clues to an English, as distinguished from a Roman, ceremonial. Liturgical texts from the patristic period were carefully studied to determine the practices in antiquity. The ritualists turned to contemporary Roman Catholic practice as well. Some of their borrowings, such as high mass without communicants and a fondness for the devotion of Benediction, have been targets for reform by a later generation of liturgiologists in the Roman Catholic Church itself.[3] It is customary nowadays to be sharply critical of many of the errors and extravagances of the ritualists, not least their taste in architecture and hymnody. Astringent criticism is required where certain aberrations still persist.[4] At the same time, we may gladly acknowledge the large contributions the Anglo-Catholic Movement has made in preparing the way for current liturgical reform and renewal.

As in biblical studies, so also in liturgical studies, an important factor continues to be the patient work of scholars from various traditions. The method of critical historical research has wrought an immense difference. Liturgical scholars have discovered a wealth of new data and are able to point to principles of corporate worship and liturgical practice which antedate and undercut many of the controversial positions adopted in the heat of conflict during the Reformation and the centuries that followed.[5] There is a widespread respect for impartial scholarship and a genuine desire in many quarters to recover principles of common prayer which may serve an ecumenical Church in an era of rapid change and social fragmentation. Partisan polemics and defensive expositions of existing rites and practices are no longer the vogue.[6]

More recent Roman Catholic thought, particularly in Germany and France, has exerted a strong influence on Anglican liturgical scholars. It has sometimes seemed that in discussions aimed at having portions of the Mass in the vernacular and "teaching masses" which seek the edification and, consequently, the greater participation of the faithful in worship, Roman Catholics were simply developing principles that had guided the Church of England in the sixteenth and seventeenth centuries. That would be a superficial judgment, however. Roman Catholic liturgical scholarship is broad and deep. The results achieved in the schema on the liturgy adopted by the Second Vatican Council in 1963 represent the cumulative efforts of generations of devoted scholars at such centers of renewal as Solesmes and Maria Laach. A casual examination of the footnotes of scholarly Anglican writers in the field, such as E. C. Ratcliff, Gregory Dix, and Massey Shepherd, testifies to the importance and influence of Roman Catholic scholarship.

Still another factor has been the stimulus of Prayer Book revision. In England, widespread discussion and study preceded the "deposited" book of 1927-28. The fiasco of its rejection by Parliament ended any hope for revision in England for a generation to come. The very bitterness of party strife at that time prepared the way for something else. Many in the Church felt an ennui, if not downright distaste, with ritualism in its sectarian expressions. Liturgical concern and discussion there was bound to be. After 1928, it seemed natural to turn to a study of liturgical principles as distinguished from specific proposals for the revision of the English Prayer Book.

The last three decades have seen the formation of one after another new province of the Anglican Communion overseas. One of the matters most frequently taken in hand by the new provinces no longer bound by the Erastian legal provisions under which the Church of England lives has been revision of the 1662 Prayer Book. The provinces of South Africa, the West Indies, and Canada, as well as the Church in India, Pakistan, Burma, and Ceylon, have all produced revisions of the 1662 book.[7] The Church of South India's liturgy is a bold and suggestive document which represents a good deal more than the revision of already existing forms. In the United States, revision was carried through in 1892 and again in 1928. A continuing Liturgical Commission has in recent years prepared an important series of *Prayer Book Studies*.[8] Dr. Massey H. Shepherd, an influential member of that commission, has recently asked whether the era of revision ought not now to be brought to a close. "The Anglican claim that its liturgy is incomparable is a silly anachronism." Dr. Shepherd continues, "No liturgy can be incomparable today unless it develops in creative response both to the finest insights of historical, liturgical scholarship, and to the relevant spiritual needs of contemporary man who is trembling on the threshold of a fundamental transition in the history of the world." [9] He proposes accordingly that a future Prayer Book, in the United States at least, should represent the consensus of liturgical scholarship and needs in those churches seriously concerned to find common forms of liturgical worship in an ecumenical era. It is Dr. Shepherd's conviction that the cause of unity would be immeasurably strengthened if Christians of various churches could grow together through the use of substantially similar, if not common, forms of worship. For the present, it remains to be seen whether this imaginative and prophetic proposal will win acceptance among the Presbyterian, Methodist, and Lutheran churches, as well as in the Episcopal Church. So far, it seems to have passed largely without notice and serious discussion. Meanwhile, the concern for liturgical renewal is being brought to the attention of the American Church through the various publications and conferences of "Associated Parishes," of which Dr. Shepherd is a guiding light and inspiration.[10]

The destruction wrought by World War II, and the large-scale movements of population to urban areas, along with the religious "boom" and affluence in the United States in the last several decades, have resulted in the building of many new churches in England and the United States as well as overseas.

This period of church building has stimulated serious thinking about what a church building is for and how best it can be designed to fill the liturgical needs of a congregation in the modern world. This, in turn, has driven many a new congregation, unfettered by an older building and the weight of past practice, to ask basic questions about the nature and principles of liturgical worship itself.[11] A. H. Couratin has rightly observed that "in no other branch of theology has interest increased in the last twenty-one years (1939-1960) as it has in Liturgy. The number of scholars, professional and amateur, working in this field is probably about as it always was. . . . But the interest of ordinary people in the subject is very much greater than ever before." [12]

Outstanding Contributions

In one sense, the story of liturgical renewal in Anglican circles might be told in terms of the steadily widening influence of a few seminal books. The first is A. G. Hebert's *Liturgy and Society,* published in 1935. It is difficult to realize that it was written three decades ago, because the book has been continuously in print and, in some respects, is as timely today as it ever was. Aware of the liturgical renewal taking place in portions of the Roman Catholic Church on the Continent and perceiving its significance as few in England did at the time, Fr. Hebert sought to direct attention to the fresh developments. It was not liturgical practices which fired his imagination, but the principles of liturgical renewal. What began in his mind as a report on significant developments elsewhere assumed a broader perspective as the book took form. "I began," he tells us, "to plan a book that would show how Christian dogma finds its typical expression in worship, and how the Christian religion is not merely a way of piety for the individual soul, but is in the first place a participation in a common life. But the subject would not allow itself to be limited to a purely religious and ecclesiastical treatment." [13] The focus broadened.

Liturgy cannot be understood apart from its social and economic implications and its expressions in art, architecture, and music. Moreover, Fr. Hebert became convinced that in the liturgy are enshrined those principles which must lie at the root of any genuinely Christian society. Significantly, the subtitle of the book is "The Function of the Church in the Modern World." Fr. Hebert speaks of "the liturgical way," of men called into an imperfect human fellowship which nonetheless lives "from age to age by the common Catholic, universal faith in God's saving work which liturgy illustrates and proclaims in a variety of ways. . . . There is no promise here of ready-made solutions for difficulties of belief, of morals, or of social life, but only of a share in a common faith and a common conflict against evil, and of help in the conflict." [14] Many a person sickened by the excesses of partisan strife, and bored by the pedantry and archaism of much discussion of liturgical matters, found that *Liturgy and Society* opened new vistas for him. Here was a book that insisted that liturgy had to do with men and the principles by which the life of society was ordered. It had to do with life on the street as well as what was done in the sanctuary. That note was altogether salutary.

In 1937, a second book important for Anglican liturgical renewal appeared: *The Parish Communion*. The name of A. G. Hebert appeared as editor and contributor of an important essay. Once more the basic theological orientation was clearly stated. For the contributors, the editor insists, "The real question is not of the best arrangement of the Sunday service, but rather of a deepened understanding of the Sacrament and of the Church." [15] The volume was written by a group of like-minded Anglo-Catholic clergy of the Church of England, among them Gregory Dix and Austin Farrer. Yet, it was not designed to be a partisan book. "We have longed," writes its editor, "to be able to do something to increase and deepen the unity of the Church of England, believing that her true unity is a spiritual unity centered round the Gospel of Redemption and the Evangelical Sacraments, and that the spread of the Parish Communion will do much to further the realization of that unity." [16] Parish communion meant, of course, a celebration of the Holy Communion at a reasonably early hour on Sunday morning, followed by a simple shared breakfast and, if possible, a meeting of the parish devoted to discussion of the implications of their common worship for their own lives, their community, and the world at large. This was proposed as the norm, wherever possible, for the chief service of worship each Sunday in a parish church. The book itself would not have been possible without the considerable parochial experience which lay behind many of the essays. Its contributors wrote about what they already knew and had experienced. Its importance lies in its clear enunciation of certain basic principles, its sound scholarship, and the persuasive way in which its central convictions are set forth. The book and the movement to whose ideas it gave an early expression have had a wide influence, perhaps chiefly in the years following World War II. Certainly, Fr. Hebert was right about one thing. The "Parish and People" movement has been a unifying factor in the English Church. Its principles and practices belong to no "party" in the traditional sense.

Dom Gregory Dix is the man more responsible than anyone else for the revival of liturgical interest in Anglican circles since the war. *The Shape of the Liturgy* appeared in 1945, and ever since has had a wide influence. Fr. Hebert had spoken of a "liturgical way." Gregory Dix made a similar point in a memorable passage. In contrast to the dissatisfied "Aquisitive Man" and his successor, the dehumanized "Mass Man," Christianity sets the "Eucharistic Man," that is,

. . . man giving thanks with the product of his labours upon the gifts of God, and daily rejoicing with his fellows in the worshipping society which is grounded in eternity. This is man to whom it was promised on the night before Calvary that he should henceforth eat and drink at the table of God and be a king. This is not only a more joyful and more humane ideal. It is the divine and only authentic conception of the meaning of all human life and its realization is in the eucharist.[17]

A. H. Couratin has described the book as "untidy" and "uneven," pointing out that more cautious scholars have found in it much with which they disagree. "But," he continues, "by its exuberance and vividness and verve it has sold liturgical study to numbers of readers who have been left untouched by writers more sober in style and in judgment." [18] E. L. Mascall is a good deal less restrained in his appraisal and speaks of the book as having "transformed Anglican liturgiology almost overnight . . . into a study whose immediate relevance became evident to multitudes of parish priests." The reason, Dr. Mascall believes, lies in the fact that its author was not only a liturgical scholar but a sacramental theologian as well, interested not only in the way worship was conducted but in the inner nature of the worship itself. "The close connection that now exists between theologians and liturgists in the Anglican Church is largely Dix's legacy." [19] Whatever the final appraisal of *The Shape of the Liturgy* may be, it has had an extraordinary influence in the last several decades.

There are numerous examples of those who have followed Dom Gregory Dix in the attempt to bring the results of liturgical scholarship to a larger popular audience. Representative of this interest are Colin Dunlop's *Anglican Public Worship* (1953), Basil Minchin's series *Worship in the Body of Christ* (1958 ff.), and Alfred B. Shands's *The Liturgical Movement and the Local Church* (1965). Frequently, liturgical concern combines with the fruits of biblical theology, as in C. F. D. Moule's *Worship in the New Testament* (1961), Reginald Fuller's *What Is Liturgical Preaching?* (1956), and J. A. T. Robinson's *Liturgy Coming to Life* (1960), together with several chapters in *On Being the Church in the World* (1960), notably those on matter, power, and liturgy. The theology of worship has been ably expounded by Evelyn Underhill. Her important book *Worship* (1936) has found a wide audience, by no means confined to Anglican circles, and her various collections of retreat addresses and occasional papers illustrate the continued vitality of the mystical strain in Anglican piety. The amount and quality of writing in the field of liturgy and worship are impressive and show no signs of slackening.

Liturgy and Community

Worship has to do with the reality of the Living God. It aims at being the most fitting and appropriate human response to that reality. It has been, and must continue to be, a central concern of the Church. Because it is a corporate activity of the Christian community, common (or public) worship properly aims at being inclusive rather than exclusive. It is for "all sorts and conditions of men," with all the richness and diversity which that implies.

Corporate worship properly enlists the finest expressions of the human spirit as it expresses itself not only in words but in gestures, music, architecture, indeed, in all artistic forms. If it is to be worthy of the final reality that it seeks to honor and adore, nothing cheap, tawdry, sentimental, or inferior will finally do. It is not surprising, therefore, that liturgical and artistic forms which served another generation are felt to be inadequate and in need of revision and reformation. In a Church which has not lost its vitality and its sense of the reality of worship, this will always be the case. One of the encouraging aspects of the present liturgical renewal is its disaffection with styles imitative of the past and its openness to contemporary artistic expressions.

Corporate worship makes its appeal to the whole person. One's mind is involved, to be sure, but so are one's deepest feelings as well. Moreover, a sense of the presence of God leaves the worshiper with a divine discontent as he becomes conscious of the gulf between the is-ness of himself and his situation and the ought-ness demanded by God's will and purpose. This supplies the tension for the spring of responsible and decisive moral action. Worship is first, last, and always addressed to Almighty God. No words, no thoughts, no artistic forms—however noble or venerable—are finally adequate for the task. The finest of words and artistic forms are but feeble attempts to express what, in the end, is beyond human expression. Thus, Alan Paton writes:

This kneeling, this singing, this reading from ancient books,
This acknowledgment that the burden is intolerable, this promise of amendment,
This humble access, this putting out of the hands,
This taking of the bread and wine, this return to your place not glancing about you,
This solemn acceptance and the thousand sins that will follow it, this thousand sins and the repenting of them,
This dedication and this apostasy, this apostasy and this restoration,
This thousand restorations, and this thousand apostasies,
Take and accept them all, be not affronted nor dismayed by them.
They are a net of holes to capture essence, a shell to house the thunder of the ocean,
A discipline of petty acts to catch Creation, a rune of words to hold One Living Word,
A ladder built by men of sticks and stones, whereby they hope to reach the heaven.[20]

The modern world needs to recover, or, perhaps, rediscover, the sense of the presence of the Living God in the midst of life as it is lived, of God at the very heart and core of the concerns which matter most for human life. If such a recovery is to take place, the vitality and authenticity of corporate worship is crucially important. Without such a recovery, the finest of theologies and the loftiest of ethical ideals are not likely to fire men's imaginations nor long hold their allegiance. Liturgical renewal has meant a renewed emphasis upon the sacramental principle at the heart of Christian worship, precisely this sense of the presence of the Divine Spirit in the midst of such common and essential activities as sharing, eating, and drinking; the awareness of God actively present when bread is broken and wine shared in the name of the crucified and risen Lord Jesus Christ. Moreover, sacramental worship involves the hallowing and consecrating of the "common ventures of life": work, love and marriage, sickness and health, the birth and rearing of children, and finally death itself. Precisely because of the impressive character of our technology and the combined force of those factors which drive modern man away from God, his neighbor, and finally himself, he needs the restoration of relationships, the healing, and the renewed insight and vision which worship alone affords.

The danger of sacramental worship is that it may lead to a too-ready acceptance of the status quo. This takes place when a vivid awareness of God's presence in the midst of human life is not combined with the deep awareness of God as other than man, that is, of God's transcendence. Thus, awe and reverence are an integral part of authentic Christian worship. There are many voices raised today to call the institutional church to sally forth and become the servant church. That imperative is altogether healthy and salutary. Too long have Christians been content to seek God primarily in the sanctuary or in the gaps in our scientific picture of the world and at the boundaries of human knowledge. It is in these areas, as Bonhoeffer suggests, that God is removing himself from us in order that we may learn to seek his presence in the midst of everyday life as it is lived in the modern world. At the same time, it is important to keep firmly in mind, as Kenneth E. Kirk has argued persuasively in his *Vision of God,* that Christian service in this world requires worship if it is to be authentically Christian. "Worship alone will 'disinfect our service from egoism,' " writes Dr. Kirk. "Disinterested service . . . is the only service that is serviceable; and disinterestedness comes by the life of worship alone." [21] The ideals of worship and service are "co-ordinate parts of the same ideal whole." Furthermore, if the Church is truly to serve the modern world, it cannot accommodate itself both to the status quo and to the assumptions which shape the modern mind, remaining, meanwhile, unaware of the tension between the *is* of the present and the *ought* of God's will and purpose. One recalls the failures in prophecy of the Church in the last one hundred years.[22] Prophecy springs from a vivid sense of God's transcendent holiness and otherness. Without that note, sacramental worship easily degenerates into a genial cultured sanctification of the status quo.

Some Caveats

Liturgical renewal has meant a renewed stress upon the Church as a community. The personal and corporate aspects of the Christian life have been stressed as over against any narrowly individualistic notions of worship. Worship has come to be regarded as a common activity of the whole body, essential for the life of its members. Stress upon congregational participation has meant a growing awareness that worship is corporate activity done *by* the worshiping community together, and not something simply done *for* them and at which they can afford to be passive spectators. As such, it requires preparation, joyful celebration, and sacrifice or wholehearted offering.[23] It is heartening to note the trend toward greater simplicity in order to encourage the full participation of those who have neither the time nor inclination for the intricacies of liturgical archaeology. The willingness to experiment with evening and home celebrations of the liturgy is refreshing. The emphasis upon relevance to the concerns of worshipers further encourages their wholehearted participation. Particularly heartening is the fact that the note of mission to the world is steadily moving to the forefront in the minds of those most concerned, as is evidenced by such titles as *Liturgy Is Mission* and *Mission and Communication*.

Insofar as the liturgical movement has shown itself responsive to constructive criticism of certain of its emphases,[24] it affords solid ground for hope for further renewal. At the same time, however, it must be noted that liturgical reform to date has been almost exclusively a clerical matter. Unlike the laity, clergy are likely to feel at home in the church building and at ease in the midst of ancient and often archaic rites and ceremonies. To better understand and more fully utilize the resources of the Christian tradition in the public worship of the Church is a subject of absorbing interest for the clerical mind. It must be recorded, however, that so far, the impact of the liturgical movement upon the great masses of men and women who rarely, if ever, enter the doors of a church has been minimal. Even when there have been changes of emphasis in ceremonial and teaching, when the very rites themselves have been revised, the typical twentieth-century man finds his interest unaroused. Faced by the numbing indifference of the vast majority of his potential flock, many a parson, once an enthusiastic devotee of liturgical renewal, finds his enthusiasm waning. To observe this is not to suggest that his previous enthusiasm was misplaced. Liturgical reform and renewal we must have. Yet taken alone, as an exclusive preoccupation, it leads to further clericalism, self-preoccupation, and disillusionment. For the problems which the Church faces in the modern world are much too intricate and deep-rooted to be met by any single avenue of approach.

CHAPTER 5

The Hesitant Quest for Unity

THE ecumenical movement is a central feature of Christian thought and concern in the twentieth century. Together with biblical theology and liturgical renewal, it has been a matter of absorbing concern for theologians and leaders of the various churches alike. The history of the movement has been told often and well from several perspectives.[1] The steadily growing volume of literature dealing with various aspects of the quest for unity among Christians has by now reached staggering proportions. To survey and discuss in any detail even the Anglican contributions of the last three decades requires a treatment of book length.[2] The intention of this chapter is to comment selectively on certain broad features of the movement which are sometimes obscured in the more detailed discussion of specific theological issues or of proposals for actual union between churches, then to seek to assess the general direction of Anglican discussion and participation in the movement during the last quarter-century, and, finally, to distinguish certain continuing problems and unresolved issues posed by the movement.

A Summary of Developments

It is important to recall at the outset the overwhelming theological imperative in the quest for unity among Christians. Christian faith proclaims a basis for unity among men which transcends race, color, ethnic, economic, or social divisions. "There is neither Jew nor Greek, there is neither slave nor free, there is neither male nor female; for you are all one in Christ

74

Jesus" (Gal. 3:28, RSV). The Lambeth Appeal for Reunion (1920) reads in part:

> We believe that God wills fellowship. By God's own act this fellowship was made, in and through Jesus Christ. We believe that it is God's purpose to manifest this fellowship, so far as this world is concerned, in an outward, visible and united society, holding one faith, having its own recognised officers, using God-given means of grace, and inspiring all its members to the world-wide service of the Kingdom of God. . . . The vision which arises before us is that of a Church genuinely Catholic, loyal to all Truth, and gathering into its fellowship all who profess and call themselves Christians, within whose visible unity all the treasures of faith and order, bequeathed as a heritage by the past to the present, shall be possessed in common and made service-able to the whole Body of Christ. . . . It is through a rich diversity of life and devotion that the unity of the whole fellow-ship will be fulfilled. . . . We do not ask that any one Com-munion should consent to be absorbed in another. We do ask that all should unite in a new and great endeavor to recover and manifest to the world the unity of the Body of Christ for which he prayed.[3]

The ecumenical movement has been and is inspired by those who are convinced that God wills unity in Christ for his Church and that to acquiesce in "our unhappy divisions" is a scandal to the Lord of the Church as well as to the world.

One of the significant contributions of the Hebrew prophets to the intellectual and moral heritage of Western man was their unshakable conviction that God is continually active in the processes of history. For the prophets, God's will and purpose for mankind are to be discovered by participation in, and re-flection upon, the historical events of the day. Although the Christian will wish to speak cautiously about the will and purpose of God disclosed in contemporary events, recalling the ease with which men have invoked divine sanction for what turns out to be the devices and desires of their own hearts, the quest for unity among Christians clearly appears to be one of the most significant movements in the modern world for the future of the churches. The Christian Church is made up of human beings, and, consequently, it has in every period of its history exhibited divisive forces which have militated against its visible unity. What is of overwhelming significance is that, in the last fifty years, centrifugal forces, those forces making for division and disunity, have been counterbalanced and offset by an even stronger centripetal force, drawing Christians into greater unity with one another.

To the impatient, the progress seems painfully slow and inconclusive. When one recalls the long history which has led to the present state of division among Christians, the overwhelming fact is that the momentum away from the center and toward an ever-increasing number of separate and competing churches has been decisively checked in the present century and replaced by a movement back toward the center of unity in Christ. So far, this has resulted in the uniting of various groups which share a common history and tradition; for example, Methodist groups coming together to form a more inclusive Methodist body. A similar phenomenon has taken place among Lutherans and Presbyterians. More adventuresome have been unions which bring together various bodies of similar traditions and backgrounds such as the union of Presbyterians, Methodists, and Congregationalists in the United Church of Canada. The Church of South India is of particular importance in that for the first time episcopal and nonepiscopal traditions have come together to form a united church.

Alongside of the various unions and mergers which have taken place in recent decades, the three-pronged thrust of faith and order, life and work, and missionary concern, after a series of memorable international conferences beginning in 1910, has culminated in the World Council of Churches, which came into being in 1948. The World Council neither is, nor purports to be, a substitute for the "coming great church." The breadth of its membership was significantly enlarged at New Delhi by the inclusion of further Orthodox bodies and several groups of Pentecostal churches. The measure of cooperation and opportunities for dialogue that it represents is a measure of the distance traveled along the road toward organic unity in the present century. The change in climate from 1910 to the present, and the possibilities opened up for mutual understanding and cooperative effort among Christians, are nothing short of astonishing.

A similar judgment must be made about the Roman Catholic Church. It has been one of the points of criticism of the ecumenical movement in its earlier phases that it seemed headed in the direction of becoming merely a Pan-Protestant movement. To outside observers, the Roman Catholic Church seemed to stand aside, aloof and unchanged in its attitude toward its "separated brethren." The ferment of ecumenism was at work in the Roman Church as well, however. When one recalls the prevailing atmosphere as late as the early 1950's, and contrasts it with the change in climate of which the reign of John XXIII and the Second Vatican Council are symbolic, one is once more struck with the distance traversed in the space of a few short years. Possibilities for mutual cooperation and dialogue have been opened up and are being utilized. This seemed out of the question a decade ago. In spite of all the difficulties, disappointments, and frustrations which undoubtedly lie ahead, the difference in climate as far as relations among Christians is concerned, in the last fifty years, is nothing short of astonishing. The accomplishments, meager though they may seem in the light of the goal to be realized, are nevertheless considerable. They are due to the devoted labor of countless men in all traditions. May we not also see in the movement toward Christian unity the presence and activity of the Holy Spirit of God? Many a pet scheme of men has been tried and found wanting, but the steady movement back toward the center of unity continues. Those most deeply committed to the goal of unity are convinced that they stand on God's side and are participating in his cause, however hesitant they may be about this or that particular step to be taken.

The practical imperatives for unity are overwhelming. Because the rate of population growth is greatest in those areas of the world where the Christian Church is weakest as far as numbers are concerned, the proportion of Christians to the total population of the world is gradually declining, and seems likely to continue to do so, in spite of the best efforts of the churches in their missionary and evangelistic endeavors. The duplication of effort in educational and evangelistic work and in social witness, particularly in Europe and North America, is hardly consistent with a faith which teaches the stewardship of time, talents, and economic resources. In Africa and Asia, resurgent rival religions and strongly nationalist governments make it abundantly clear that the time during which Christians could enjoy the luxury of a divided Church is rapidly running out. Where Christians are only a tiny minority of the total population, the anachronism of a divided Church is painfully apparent and a serious handicap. Everywhere in the world, the Christian faith is being called to face, and deal creatively with, the secularism which has accompanied rapid industrialization and mass urbanization. Humanly speaking, a divided Church seems quite unequal to such a task, however heroically parts of the Church here and there seek to meet the challenge of their mission.

To an extent not always appreciated by theologians, modern science and technology have provided the "hardware" which must make the isolation of the various churches incompatible with life in the twentieth century. Rapid communication and travel have dramatically reduced distances around the world. It is possible now to travel to most parts of Europe, Africa, or Asia in less time than it once took a country parson on horseback to make his rounds on a given Sunday. London or Ibadan or Bombay is closer to the major cities in the United

States by air than many a rural town was to its state capital a generation ago. Modern means of communication make it possible for ideas, even theological ideas, to be disseminated almost instantaneously. The sense of urgency in the quest for unity, felt so keenly by the Christian of Africa and Asia, is increasingly being heard in the deliberations of the World Council of Churches and at the sessions of the Vatican Council as indigenous leadership replaces European and American leadership among the "younger churches." Popular education is steadily raising the level of literacy and understanding around the world. In many an area, and not alone overseas, the pulpit has fallen behind the pew as patterns of theological education have failed to keep pace with the rapid rise in education and understanding among lay people. The tides of history are running in the direction of greater mutual understanding and cooperation in nearly every area of human endeavor. This does not mean that the future of the ecumenical movement is unclouded, or that the fruition of the hopes and dreams of so many for the "coming great church" will be easily realized. It does mean that the modern world provides opportunities for mutual cooperation and understanding, based on first-hand knowledge and experience, which was impossible a few decades ago.

In its initial stages, there was some ground for the suspicion that the ecumenical movement was symptomatic of a certain decay in Protestant theology and that one reason large areas of agreement in theological matters could hopefully be charted was that, for many participants, no theological issues were of supreme importance. In Roman Catholic quarters, there was a strong suspicion, at least initially, that the movement was but another expression of the modernism condemned in 1907 by Pope Leo XIII. It is significant, therefore, to point out that during the last three decades the movement has gone forward in the midst of an important theological revival associated with the names of Karl Barth, Emil Brunner, Paul Tillich, and

Reinhold Niebuhr. On the side of faith and order, there has been little disposition to settle for a minimizing type of theology. In 1947, the report *Catholicity,* prepared by a group of Catholic-minded Anglicans, pointed out that "conflict has arisen from the loss of an original wholeness, and a resulting distortion of categories." [4] The report catalogues the cost of schism and isolation within the Church and is sharply critical of seeking to remedy the situation by fastening broken pieces together, by seeking an agreed basis for "our common Christianity" or by separating matters of faith and matters of order. It stresses that there is a givenness about the Church and its unity into which all Christians are called. The way to unity is a way of recovery of the wholeness and unity given in Christ and his Church. "The true way of synthesis is not to take our contemporary systems or 'isms' or Church traditions and try to piece them together, either as a whole or in selected items, but rather to go behind our contemporary systems and strive for the recovery of the fullness of Tradition within the thought and worship and order and life of each of the sundered portions of Christendom." [5] Participation in faith-and-order discussions has, on the whole, deepened the theological awareness of the participants, making them aware that the truth is greater than any single conception of it and strengthening the desire to recover that wholeness which Christ wills for his Church and which cannot fully be realized in isolation from other Christians. [6]

This sense that participation in the quest for unity involves in some sense a recovery of a wholeness that no church manifests fully in the present has been strengthened by the work of biblical and liturgical scholars. As we have seen, biblical theology and liturgical renewal in the present century have helped to build a basis of mutual understanding and sympathy that dramatically cuts across older ecclesiastical and theological differences. The international community of scholarship which has come into being quietly and without fanfare or elaborate programs has worked to break down isolation and parochialism. "What is most interesting is that many of the growing points in ecumenical discussion for a new and more united understanding of the truth of the gospel have been found . . . where scholars have been prepared to push behind the attitudes of the Middle Ages and to discover a synthesis which is altogether different from a simple compromise between two opposing points of view," writes A. M. Allchin. "We are beginning to get behind the problems of the Reformation and the Counter-Reformation, and to find a synthesis which is greater than either." [7]

Theology has been immensely enriched by the fact of the ecumenical movement and the discussions which have surrounded it. Increasingly, theologians in most traditions consciously address their colleagues and prospective readers across denominational lines. There is a recognizable body of theological writing which has come into being as a direct result of ecumenical gatherings and the discussions which have preceded and followed them.[8] The Roman Catholic Church has shown the greatest interest in small groups of theologians gathering for theological dialogue in depth. Such dialogue is giving rise to a significant and growing body of material which renders many a generalization about Protestants and Catholics alike entirely out of date. Whether or not the twentieth century will prove to be the century in which Christians reach a deeper level of understanding of the nature of the Church, as the fifth century proved to be the century for clarifying the nature of the person of Christ, the fact of the ecumenical movement itself is of the greatest importance for the theologian. The opportunities for dialogue and the cumulative work of scholars and theologians have created a situation in which there remains little excuse for that isolation and parochialism which has limited the results of theological work in the past. No doubt the road ahead will prove very much longer and more arduous than most imagine at the present time. Many a cherished conviction will have to be radically revised and reformulated in the light of scrutiny by those who approach it with a degree of objectivity impossible for one who has long been confined in a particular ecclesiastical or theological tradition. The fact to be reckoned with is that an entirely new climate is coming into being. Whether the churches and their theologians can seize and utilize the opportunities before them in an era of ecumenism only time can tell, and, humanly speaking, time is running out.

Anglican Approaches

Charles Gore (1853-1932), perhaps the leading Anglo-Catholic Churchman and theologian of his generation, wryly remarked of himself, "Someone has been good enough to say of me that, though I have a great zeal for reunion, no one is a greater obstacle to its realization." [9] A similar judgment might be made about the Anglican Communion generally. The quest for unity has proven to be a hesitant quest. On the one hand, the contributions of Anglicans to the cause of Christian unity have been impressive. One need only recall the leadership of such men as Charles H. Brent, A. C. Headlam, William Temple, G. K. A. Bell, Stephen Neill, Oliver Tompkins, and a host of others over the last half-century, or such documents as the Lambeth Appeal of 1920 and subsequent Lambeth Conference Reports, particularly those of 1930 and 1948. More recently, Edward R. Hardy, John Knox, W. Norman Pittenger, and William Nicholls played important roles in the preparation and final formulation of the statement on faith and order in Montreal. In England, Kenneth Riches and Sidney Greenslade have played important roles in the meetings on faith and order. Close and continuing relationships have been established with the Old Catholic Churches, the Swedish Lutheran Church, the Polish National Catholic Church, and the Philippine Independent Church—looking toward a meaningful unity and mutual cooperation in a "Wider Episcopal Fellowship." [10] In each case, closer relations have been established with churches which have maintained an episcopal polity and the principle of Apostolic Succession. In addition, the constituent provinces of the Anglican Communion have taken an active role in support of the activities of the World Council of Churches. Provinces of the Anglican Communion are presently involved in discussions looking toward reunion with fellow Christians in India, Ceylon, Nigeria, the United States, and in England, to mention only those areas where discussions are currently moving forward toward definite proposals for reunion in the foreseeable future.[11]

At the same time, there is a significant body of Anglican opinion which feels strongly that, at this juncture, concrete schemes for reunion are premature. Discussions between Anglicans and Presbyterians, which culminated in specific proposals in the United States in 1946 and in Scotland in the late fifties, failed resoundingly to win approval when they passed from the negotiating committees to the churches as a whole. The record of Anglican response to the Church of South India should give pause to any undue optimism about proposals currently under discussion.[12]

The plain fact is that Anglicans themselves are deeply divided over the nature of the Church and the question of whether its polity is a matter of "fundamentals," and thus essential to its very being, or whether it is an "accessory," of the greatest importance to the well-being and fullness of the Church's life, but ultimately a matter secondary to the gospel itself. The Lambeth Appeal of 1920 commended episcopacy as a treasured aspect of the Anglican heritage and important as a part of the fullness of a united Church, while at the same time being careful to assert its belief in the efficacy and spiritual benefits with which God had blessed the labors of ministries not episcopally ordained.[13] If the language of the Appeal gave rise to misunderstandings in some Protestant quarters, discussion in the next several years made it abundantly clear that the Anglican Communion would insist upon episcopacy as the *sine qua non* of any serious proposal for re-union. The point had been effectively made, even if its theological justification remains fully to be clarified. Lambeth 1930 made significant strides in this direction in the context of the beginnings of serious conversations which were to bear fruit in the Church of South India a quarter of a century later. The Anglican Communion has made it clear that it is itself wholeheartedly committed to the threefold ministry, centering in the historic episcopate and to the pattern of sacramental worship provided by such a ministry.

The view that episcopacy belongs to the essence of the Church was expounded at length and with great learning in *The Apostolic Ministry* (1946), edited by Kenneth E. Kirk, then Bishop of Oxford. "The Episcopate," wrote Dr. Kirk, "is the divinely ordained ministerial instrument for securing to the Church of God its continuous and organic unity as a God-given city of salvation." [14] "The Apostles were not only witnesses of the Resurrection; they were also stewards, ministers, rulers. And if that office was necessary in the Church of the first generation . . . , a like function was necessary in the Church of every succeeding generation." [15] The bishop is the successor of the Apostles; the episcopate is the *essential ministry;* only those within the succession can admit others. Dom Gregory Dix, in the same volume, writes, "The Episcopate is the only means by which our Lord's own commission to stand in His Person before God and man is given afresh to each new minister of His Church (according to His own order) to the end of time." [16] The practical consequence of this view is that "we shall be forced to regard as unscriptural and unapostolic any suggestion of extending even for a limited period the right of consecrating and ordaining in the Church of God to those who do not stand in the line of authenticated succession from the Essential Ministry of the earliest times. Equally unscriptural and unapostolic is the view that the ministry of word and sacraments in the Church of Christ can be legitimately exercised by any who have not received the commission to do so from the same unimpeachable source." [17] A further consequence is that the continuity of the Church depends solely upon the continuity of its ministry. "Should [the] ministry fail," writes Dr. Kirk, "the apostolic Church, which is the Body of Christ in space and time, would disappear with it." [18] The case for the Tractarian view of the Church, the necessity for episcopacy, and for valid sacraments by a ministry episcopally ordained was argued with great skill and ingenuity, particularly by such contributors as Gregory Dix, Austin Farrer, and A. G. Hebert. The book received a decidedly mixed reaction and has been sharply criticized on both historical and theological grounds.[19] It remains the most formidable exposition of the Tractarian and Anglo-Catholic view of the issues, and, in a preface to a subsequent edition, Austin Farrer expresses the conviction, shared by many a Catholic-minded Anglican, that criticisms of the book have done little to shake the belief of its contributors that its fundamental positions remain secure.[20]

This is not the place to trace in detail the finer points of the discussion of the Church and the ministry among Anglicans during the last several decades. Out of the continuing debate, several points emerge with increasing clarity. The point of view championed by the Tractarians, by Bishop Gore, and, more recently, by *The Apostolic Ministry,* together with the writings of A. L. Peck and E. L. Mascall, has undergone some minor modifications and refinements.[21] Insufficient weight has been placed on the fact that a doctrine of such far-reaching consequences requires a basis firmer than what is at best a probable reconstruction of the historical evidence. Bishop Newbigin of South India puts the matter thus: "When a man speaks to us of the things which he deems so vital to the redemption of the world that he places them alongside the Gospel, and demands in their name the excommunication of great parts of Christ's Church . . . , we are in a realm where probability is not enough. Here, we need something as sure as the Cross and the empty tomb." [22]

The Tractarian position has been advanced and defended with great skill and erudition by successive generations of theologians. There have been times when it appeared to be *the* Anglican position, a view to which its champions would whole-heartedly subscribe. It has singularly failed to convince the Anglican Communion as a whole, however. It has been re-peatedly pointed out that although Anglicans are committed to the fact of episcopacy, the meaning of that fact and the prac-tical consequences to be drawn from it need not be those drawn by the defenders of the Tractarian position.[23] There is a significant body of opinion in the Church which, although it values episcopacy and would strongly insist upon its necessity in a reunited Church, shows no disposition to be pushed to the lengths of saying "no bishop, no church." As one contribu-tor to *The Historic Episcopate* (1954) has put it:

In the episcopate is embodied alike the dependence of every congregation upon the one Church of God, of which it is but a local manifestation, and the continuity of the whole in doctrine, liturgy and authority with the historic events in which it was founded. Every scheme for Christian unity must come to terms with the historic episcopate; for *despite* it the Church cannot in fact be fully one, catholic or apostolic. . . . But what we are concerned to deny (as unbiblical, unhistorical and unanglican) is a particular interpretation of the episcopate which would automatically unchurch any part of the Body that for historical reasons has failed to preserve it. For that is to exalt it as a pre-condition of the Church, whereas the only precondition of the Church is the Kingdom of God. We affirm that the episcopate is dependent on the Church, and not the Church on the episcopate. We believe its possession to be a necessary mark of the Church's fullness, rather than an indispensable qualification for being a part. It is not what makes the Church the Church—so that in exclusion from it everything falls to the ground. But in repudiation of it the Church can never express the plenitude of its being as the one Body of Christ in history.[24]

The point must be put with firmness. The Anglo-Catholic, or Tractarian, position is not *the* position of the Anglican Communion, but only one of several held within its bounds. Although it has been defended with the utmost skill and learning, it has not put its alternatives to flight, nor does it seem likely to. When it is said that the Anglican Communion is committed to the fact of episcopacy but not to any particular theory of it, it needs to be stated clearly that the particular theory in question means the Tractarian theory. The assumption that one who makes such a statement implies that he holds no view of the importance of episcopacy is altogether gratuitous and unwarranted, as men with the acumen of E. L. Mascall and Austin Farrer well know. To affirm the reality of Christ's presence in the Eucharist, although refusing to be explicit as to the precise mode of the presence, is not to regard the doctrine of Real Presence as of no account.

As long ago as 1917, T. A. Lacey advanced the idea that the whole Catholic Church was in schism, yet possessing a measure of unity of "race" in the underlying brotherhood of all baptized.[25] His idea that schism is within the Church has been developed in various interesting ways, not least by the contributors to *The Historic Episcopate,* who sought to avoid the dilemma—episcopacy is either of the *esse* or of the *bene esse* of the Church—by arguing that it belongs to the *plene esse,* or fullness of the Body, into which the "coming great church" is called to grow. The volume takes the position that episcopacy is a valued and integral part of the Anglican heritage, necessary for a reunited Church, but at the same time refuses to press its claims in such a manner as to unchurch nonepiscopally ordained ministries. Like William Temple, its contributors were prepared to countenance certain temporary anomalies and contradictions in current practice, specifically with regard to the Church of South India, in order that a basis of unity might be laid in a Church firmly committed thereafter to a ministry which would be episcopally ordained.[26]

Professor Norman Sykes, in his *Old Priest and New Presbyter* (1956), a book which is primarily historical rather than theological in its contents, examines Anglican thought and practice in the sixteenth to nineteenth centuries and finds it rather more ambiguous than the strictest Tractarian and his present-day successors might prefer. His conclusion is: "The via media affirms the maintenance of episcopacy by the Church of England as part of a continuity with the early and medieval church, its acceptance on the ground of historical continuance since the apostolic age, its requirement for ministering within its own communion, and its restoration to those churches which have lost it, as a condition of reunion, without asserting their non-episcopal ministries and sacraments to be invalid because of its loss." [27] The point in referring to such books as *The Historic Episcopate* and *Old Priest and New Presbyter* is not to imply that the positions there advanced do not in turn pose difficulties which have been examined at length by other theologians. Rather, I wish to indicate something of the vitality and vigor of a view of the ministry which, historically speaking, has far deeper roots in Anglican divinity than the position of the Tractarians. The alternative and, I would argue, the traditional position has the great advantage of not linking its advocacy of an episcopal ministry with theories of a succession of consecration and the validity of orders first developed by St. Augustine in his controversy with the Donatists in the fifth century.[28] It is an irony of Christian history that a theory concerning the validity of orders and sacraments once advanced in the interest of healing schism has now apparently become an instrument for perpetuating existing schisms within the Church.

It seems likely that the debates carried on during the forties and fifties have served their purpose and that there is little to be gained from further discussions about *esse, bene esse,* and *plene esse.* The discussion is not likely to advance further until it becomes clear to Catholics that their more evangelically and liberal-minded fellow Christians hold a strong and positive view of the place and importance of order and structure in the institutional life of the Church; and Catholics show a willingness to relate their stress upon catholic order to the gospel and to the biblical doctrine of justification by grace through faith recovered at the time of the Reformation. In this connection, it is important to note that the present Archbishop of Canterbury, Dr. Ramsey, published a seminal book, *The Gospel and the Catholic Church* (1936). If the details of Dr. Ramsey's argument do not always carry the weight he wished to place upon them,[29] the book is significant in that it represented ably that stress upon catholic order could be combined in Dr. Ramsey's case with a deep and profound awareness of the importance to the gospel itself of catholic principles of church order. Here was a combination of catholic principle and evangelical concern which opened up new vistas for fruitful discussion.[30] Dr. Ramsey's book did not bear the fruit which it might have in the years immediately following its appearance since it was a first book by a then relatively unknown younger theologian and because the outbreak of the Second World War turned men's minds to more immediate and pressing problems. It has probably been more widely read and influential in the 1950's in its second edition, published after its author had become Archbishop of York. Its fundamental insight of the vital connection between catholic order and biblical faith has not yet received the attention it deserves from Anglican writers.

A grave weakness of the Tractarian view of episcopacy lies in isolating the institution of episcopacy from its embodiment in the corporate life of the Church as a whole. As T. F. Torrance has noted, "One major effect of the Tractarian movement in severing episcopal continuity from the unity and continuity of the whole Church was to make of it, perhaps for the first time, strictly a denomination in communion neither with the Church of Rome nor the Churches of the Reformation, nor indeed with three hundred years of its own past tradition." [31] It is precisely here that William Temple—who combined a respect, indeed reverence, for the givenness of catholic order and continuity with the past with the equally profound conviction that where Christ is, there the Church is also— supplies a needed corrective. Temple refused to isolate the ministry from the Church it has been commissioned to serve. He puts the matter thus:

> When I consecrate a godly and well-learned man to the office and work of a Bishop in the church of God, I do not act as a representative of the Church, if by that is meant the whole number of contemporary Christians; but I do act as the ministerial instrument of Christ in His Body, the Church. The authority by which I act is His, transmitted to me through His apostles and those to whom they committed it; I hold it neither from the Church nor apart from the Church, but from Christ in the Church . . . . this authority to consecrate and ordain is itself witness to the continuity of the life of the Church in its unceasing dependence on its head, Jesus Christ. . . . [32]

Temple was writing of the proposed Plan of Union for the Church of South India, urging that Anglicans must not "make difficult the access of others to the Apostolic Ministry." His emphasis upon the Apostolic Ministry as the *"ministerial instrument of Christ in His Body, the Church"* supplies a sorely needed emphasis which checks the tendency toward sectarianism and denominationalism, which is implied by severing episcopacy from its embodiment in the corporate life of the Church.

An Appraisal

The quest for unity has thus far been for Anglicans a hesitant quest. Ecumenical encounter is forcing the Anglican Communion to seek to clarify its own mind as to precisely why it treasures the threefold ministry centering in the episcopate, and why it must insist upon its maintenance in a reunited Church. On the theological level, the results of the discussions to date have been somewhat inconclusive. Much of the writing has been done by those living in Britain and North America who, so far at least, simply do not feel the imperatives for unity and the scandal of schism in the way that Christians overseas feel them. A deeper grasp of the imperatives to unity and the realities of the twentieth century may make the quest somewhat less hesitant in the years to come, particularly in view of the far-reaching changes underway in the Roman Church. If the discussion is to move forward, it seems to the present writer that lines of thought marked out by Temple and Ramsey nearly three decades ago must receive more attention than they have yet received. It is altogether possible that while the theological discussion continues, events will overtake the discussions of the theologians. The Anglican Communion has demonstrated many times its preference for compromise and ecclesiastical diplomacy to the task of theological clarification.

Participation in the ecumenical movement has disclosed the temptation of the Anglican Communion toward denominationalism and confessionalism. It would, indeed, be tragic if a church which has for centuries taken seriously its vocation to be the church of an entire people succumbs to the temptation to be merely an episcopal sect. There is a real and unresolved tension between loyalty to the Anglican Communion, with its heritage of faith and worship, and wholehearted participation in the ecumenical movement. If the vision of the ecumenical movement implies that in some sense all churches must die in order to be reborn as part of a reunited Church, talk of the vocation of Anglicanism to disappear seems to many to be premature and deeply threatening at the present time. There is a long and difficult road to travel before such a vocation is widely hailed in Anglican circles. To branches of the Anglican Communion overseas, which frequently are a tiny minority of the Christians of a given country where the total number of Christians is but a small proportion of the population as a whole, participation in a world-wide fellowship of Christians that transcends national and racial barriers is a source of great strength and comfort. At the same time, this very sense of belonging to the Anglican Communion may hinder their wholehearted participation in the causes of Christian witness and cooperation with their fellow countrymen who belong to a different Christian tradition.

Discussion over the nature of the Church and its ministry has to some extent accentuated the awareness of divisions within the Anglican Communion as between Catholics, Evangelicals, and Liberals. If there has been a marked decline in the bitterness of party strife in the last three decades or more, there remain many unresolved tensions and difficulties. There is cause for a measure of sober rejoicing that the Anglican Communion itself demonstrates by its continued existence that in spite of sometimes wide doctrinal differences, there is an underlying unity capable of holding together apparently mutually conflicting points of view within one Church. The fact is significant in that it holds open the hope that by living and working together and in seeking to learn from one another, Christians may yet discover more of that unity which underlies our differences and divisions. It also suggests that common worship and mission need not await a uniformity and complete agreement upon all vexing doctrinal matters. Anglicans are scarcely in a position to demand of those with whom they may unite a greater degree of agreement on matters of faith and practice than Anglicans themselves are able to reach.

There are encouraging signs that Anglicans, in their conversations with other Christians, are discovering that it is possible to witness to their convictions while at the same time adopting a somewhat less intransigent posture. The question of intercommunion between churches seriously committed to reunion has been reopened in England by the "open letter" of thirty-two theologians, and in the United States by the House of Bishops at the General Convention which met in 1964. There appears to be real progress in the conversations leading toward reunion both in England and in the United States— although the road ahead will undoubtedly prove difficult. It is in growing together that a basis for hope in the future rests, because, as Luther once observed, "Through incessant mutual conversations of the brethren, the Word of God breaks through."

CHAPTER 6

Ministry and Mission

BIBLICAL theology, liturgical renewal, and ecumenical dialogue each in turn offer hope for the renewal of the Church in our day. At the same time, such movements, important as they are for the continuing life of the Church, are symptomatic of a certain self-preoccupation. Such movements are of absorbing interest to a portion of the faithful, chiefly the clergy. Their impact upon the "outsider" has been minimal so far. This is not surprising. Each movement points to the necessity of recovering a deeper sense of the nature of the Church and its mission to the world. Such concern, broadly speaking, has been the dominant interest of serious theological work for the past three decades.[1] It is of the utmost importance and must continue. At the same time, the "outsider" is likely to find his interest aroused initially not by discussions of what the Church *is,* but by observation of what, in fact, the Church *does.* All too often the answer appears to be, "not much that really matters" in the world of the twentieth century. A deeper understanding of what the Church is called to be may well come through examination of what it is called to do and the various relationships such a mission or vocation involves. The Church must be seen in functional and relational, as well as ontological, terms.

In 1830, E. B. Pusey wrote to a German correspondent that few theological works of consequence seemed to arise in Britain from an abstract love of investigation. "Our greatest and some immortal works have arisen in some exigencies of the times," wrote Dr. Pusey. "[They] were written not merely to solve problems of importance in themselves, but such as the

94

good of the Church in our country at that time required." [2] There is a certain *ad hoc* and occasional character about much Anglican theological work. Concern about the ominous drift away from the institutional church, which is being "thrust towards a critical point," to use Leslie Paul's phrase, has led to a lively discussion about new forms of ministry. That discussion leads naturally to a deeper grasp of the mission of the Church, and suggests that ministry and mission are functions of the whole body of the Church, laity as well as clergy. Here, as with the other movements we have been considering, the discussion cuts across traditional party and denominational lines. It has been particularly vigorous in European Roman Catholic and Protestant circles.[3] We turn now to a survey of the discussion as it has been carried on in Anglican circles, bearing in mind that it is but a part of a much broader and continuing recovery taking place in the larger Church.

Experimental vs. Exploratory Ministry

An important feature of Anglican church life is the ideal of the parish church served by its resident priest and ministering to a geographical unit immediately surrounding the church building. This is a pattern so firmly entrenched that the Church is inclined to find itself embarrassed, as occasionally happens, when confronted by a man who offers himself for ordination and at the same time is not particularly interested in, or suited for, parish work. There are more than a few who "view with alarm" the steady rise in the number of nonparochial clergy, assuming that a man not engaged in parish work is somehow turning away from the "real" ministry. The parochial pattern of ministry is admirably suited to the relatively stable and settled rural, town, and small-city environment. It has served the Church well over the centuries. It seems likely in the foreseeable future that a majority of men ordained will serve a large part, if not all, of their ministries in a parochial setting. The parochial pattern of ministry will continue, hopefully with a great deal of imaginative experimentation. It is a pattern which has demonstrated considerable flexibility and adaptability in the past and may be expected to do so in the future.[4]

At the same time, it is becoming obvious to alert and sensitive observers that many of the traditional patterns of congregational and parochial life, and a clergy largely trained to minister to people within such structures, are increasingly unable to minister effectively to masses of men and women in the highly mobile, rapidly changing technological society characteristic of the twentieth century.[5] Patterns of church life once adequate and, indeed, highly satisfactory for a more settled and stable social order no longer have the effectiveness they once had. Large numbers of people moving from a rural or town and country setting into large urban centers drift away from the institutional church as they discover that it occupies a peripheral, rather than a central, role in the life of the large urban complexes. A person moving to an urban center frequently finds his place in a sociological group which has been estranged from the institutional church for generations. In Europe and Britain at least, it has been repeatedly pointed out that the churches have not lost the allegiance of the working classes; they never really had it. Typically, a person living in a modern city resides in one community and works in quite another, frequently some distance from his home and with associates drawn from widely scattered parts of the urban complex. The bonds of interest that he shares with his fellow workers are frequently far deeper than those shared with the people who happen to occupy the houses in his neighborhood. A parish church located where he resides and ministering primarily to the needs of women, children, the elderly, and the retired is of little assistance in helping the individual to make significant connections between his faith and his work. Far-reaching decisions affecting the lives of many people and sometimes entire communities are made in centers of power and responsibility far removed from the residential communities surrounding our cities. By itself, the parish church in such a residential community is quite unable to engage in fruitful dialogue with the centers of power, "the principalities and powers," of a technological society.[6]

In the United States, a parish means not a geographical unit, but a congregation of people who worship in a particular church building. Gibson Winter has ably described the flight of many such congregations from urban blight in the inner city to the outskirts, a flight which leaves the inner city bereft of the service and influence of the Church, and at the same time encourages the isolation, homogeneity, and lack of social responsibility of congregations trapped by the "suburban captivity of the churches." [7] It goes without saying that planning and strategy on a regional and diocesan level is frequently hamstrung by the conservatism, parochialism, and congregationalism of largely autonomous individual congregations. This is not to suggest that the parish church should be abandoned. What is required is a far greater sense of responsibility and mission on the part of the Church as a whole to an entire urban complex and exploratory forms of ministry to meet the needs of those not being reached by already existing parish ministries. As Gibson Winter has recently pointed out, "residential chaplaincies to family life, . . . preoccupied with the maintenance of emotional stability and the nurture of children," will not suffice in the modern world. Such a ministry "leaves untouched the vast structures of metropolitan life that determine the shape of our world" and the people living in it.[8]

The terms "experimental" and "exploratory," as applied to ministry, illustrate significant differences in approach, both of which are required. The newsletter of the Parishfield Community, located in Brighton, Michigan, puts the matter in this way:

Experimental ministries, with all their variations, share one assumption that the essential *form* of Christian mission and ministry is known. All presuppose some kind of congregation. . . . Many of the activities may take place apart from this gathering and may involve other than members; but the congregation is the center about which all aspects of the experiment revolve.

An *exploratory ministry,* on the other hand, presupposes no forms at all. The exploration is entered into precisely because those who undertake it do not presume to know in advance what structures appropriate to ministry in the urban-industrial complex may be. They set out to explore the metropolitan complex (for example) as objectively as possible, seeking any evidence of ministry being performed there, prepared to acknowledge free and responsible servanthood in whatever form it may be found. . . .[9]

The newsletter points out that the danger any exploratory ministry faces is the demand of the institutional church "for structure and results." It is often a lonely and agonizing business to find oneself a pioneer in a strange land that few of one's associates seem interested in exploring. The report concludes with three searching questions:

(1) Can the organized church afford to let some of its members engage in exploratory ministries while maintaining their "good standing" in the institution? (2) Can exploratory ministries be effectively carried on as functions of the institution? (3) Have we been right in assuming that, still in our time, some form of "fellowship" (*koinonia*) is indispensable to the Christian community? And, if so, *What does it look like?*

Such questions are not easily or quickly answered.

The roots of concern with exploratory forms of ministry are many and varied. It was natural for a church which had inherited, and was committed to, the parochial form of ministry to provide chaplaincies—institutional, military, or educational —to those groups that from time to time and for various reasons found themselves removed from the normal ministrations of the parochial clergy. The pattern of a chaplaincy naturally suggested a chaplain type of ministry in urban industrial centers where parochial forms of ministry had often proved ineffective for generations. Pioneering work along such lines was carried out by E. R. Wickham and his associates in the Sheffield Industrial Mission, and has been widely imitated elsewhere. Chaplaincy implies a ministry to those who, on the whole, are attached to the institutional church, although separated from its regular ministrations for a time for particular and usually temporary reasons. What began as a *chaplaincy* soon turned into an industrial *mission* because those involved found themselves working chiefly with men who had little or no vital connection with the institutional church and, in many instances, whose families had not had for generations. The distinction between the words "chaplaincy" and "mission," and the mentality that the two words imply, is all important. Chaplaincy suggests an experimental ministry, which continues to be very much needed. Mission points to exploratory forms of ministry, as yet largely unformed and untried. The experience of the Sheffield Industrial Mission, the Parishfield Community, and the Detroit Industrial Mission has led them toward exploratory ministries and to a renewed sense of mission which is beginning to percolate through portions of the Church. The experience of the Evangelical Lay Academies on the Continent, the new religious communities such as Iona and Taizé, and the writings of the French worker-priests have all had their influence upon the continuing discussion and exploration of new and more appropriate expressions of ministry and mission.[10]

Whether a sense of the urgent need for fresh and imaginative forms will overcome the innate conservatism of the institutional church remains to be seen. Certainly the need for the reform of existing structures and for bold experimentation is clear and pressing.[11] Whether, in addition, the institutional church can find within itself the resources to give support and sympathetic encouragement to its sons and daughters who find themselves called to new and quite untraditional expressions of mission only time can tell. The Spirit stirs those whom God chooses both within and without the bounds of the institutional structures inherited from the past. If the Church is in any measure to fulfill its calling in the modern world, it must be prepared to allow the forms of its ministry to be shaped by the needs of those it is called into being to serve.[12]

Ministry Today

The ordained ministry has been described as "the perplexed profession." It is cause for genuine concern that the number of men presenting themselves for ordination is barely adequate to meet the present needs of the Church, thereby permitting little leeway for experimental and exploratory ministries. Moreover, there is the strong suspicion that the Church is not attracting its share of the unusually gifted men that it requires for its leadership in the years to come.[13] It is certainly the case that many of the ablest men in the ordained ministry are raising searching questions about the effectiveness of their work and the existing forms within which they feel obliged to serve. Some go so far as to question whether they themselves were truly called to ordination and can best serve God and his purpose by continuing to function as clergymen. If the reasons behind such perplexity and frustration are always personal, varied, and complex, nevertheless they cry out for some discussion. The present writer has himself served for some years as a parish priest and more recently has devoted ten years of his life to theological education. Consequently, he feels much sympathy with the complexity of the task that the ordained clergyman encounters and with the ensuing tensions and perplexities that he must live with and try to see his way through to creative solutions.

What are some of the roots of the perplexity? Several writers have noted that the institutional church exhibits certain characteristics of the dinosaur and the battleship. New forms of church life to meet the needs of a rapidly changing social order are urgently needed. The task of seeking to help men to become reconciled with God and one another is one that only a man deeply devoted—and even a bit mad?—is prepared to undertake in his most exuberant and optimistic moments. To be saddled with the burden of structures and forms from the past which the Church is extraordinarily reluctant to jettison or revamp and reform makes a difficult task doubly burdensome.

The sociologist David Riesman has noted that one of the dominant characteristics of contemporary American life is the emergence of what he calls the "outer-directed individual," that is, one who derives his self-image and sense of identity almost exclusively in terms of the expectations of others.[14] The modern clergyman, with his radar set carefully tuned to the many and conflicting expectations of others, often finds that he has little or no sense of personal identity. In striving "to be all things to all men," and to please God as well, he discovers that the resulting tensions and conflicts are almost more than he can bear. Not infrequently, he breaks down emotionally under the strains. The problem is compounded by the unrealistic expectations for himself and others which many a man brings to the work of the ordained ministry.[15] The surprising fact is not that some men snap under the strain, but that many more do not do so.

To an extraordinary degree, the clergyman is expected to be a jack of all trades and master of most. He is asked to be preacher, pastor, prophet, administrator, educator, counselor, social worker—the list extends almost indefinitely. He knows in his saner moments that he can do many tasks passably well and some few with unusual skill upon occasion. At the same time, the demands upon him have a way of outrunning his capacities, no matter how able and gifted he may be. He finds himself living in an era which places a high value on specialized knowledge and technical competence. Gone is the day when amiability and good intentions would suffice to see him through most situations. A cheery smile and an exhortation to "take it to the Lord in prayer" seem inadequate in the face of most, if not all, of the social and pastoral problems with which he is called to deal. People are used to turning to the "expert" on matters of real importance: to the doctor for medical care; to an accountant for tax problems; to the psychiatrist for emotional and marital conflicts; to sociologists and social psychologists for problems in community relations and planning. The day of the gifted amateur in the ordained ministry is passing, and this is as it should be.

It is the fashion to criticize the seminaries and theological colleges for their failure to prepare men fully for the ensuing ministry. Undoubtedly, there is much that can and should be set right as far as theological education is concerned. The root of the matter lies deeper, however, in the naïve assumption that it is possible to give a man the education that the canons of the Church anticipate in the academic disciplines of biblical interpretation, church history, theology, ethics, the history and conduct of liturgical worship, preaching, and pastoral care, and, at the same time, to impart the sort of technical competence in Christian education, pastoral counseling, and the administration of an institutional parish, which can be acquired only through some years of practical experience, all in the space of two or three years. [16] Moreover, the theological scene itself is shifting with remarkable rapidity. It is worth reflection that the writings of Paul Tillich; Dietrich Bonhoeffer; most of Bultmann, including the famous essay on "demythologization"; and all the later Karl Barth were unknown to English-speaking theological students twenty years ago. A man relying on the knowledge and skills learned in seminary to carry him through a life-long ministry is defeated before he begins. This is simply to point out what is the case in law, medicine, teaching, or social work—namely, that a man's professional training is only the beginning of a continuing process of education which properly lasts throughout his life. Urgently needed is a wider understanding of what the seminaries and theological colleges are equipped to do, and cannot do, coupled with a continuing program of postordination education and training. This should undoubtedly begin immediately after ordination with an internship as part of a team ministry, during which time a man would be encouraged to develop his particular abilities in one or more specialized areas of the work of the ministry for his own sake, the good of the team, and the needs of the people he is called to serve. Hopefully, a man might learn both the need to turn to others more expert than himself as particular problems requiring special competence arise, and the habit of seeking to mobilize the total resources of the entire Church in a given community rather than trying to muddle through all alone. Such an experience would help to counteract the isolation that many a clergyman experiences and the feeling that he has been cast alone and ill-prepared into a job with which no man can reasonably cope. Continuing on-the-job training by means of seminars, workshops, conferences, and the discussion of case studies with his peers should be the rule throughout a man's active ministry.[17] If it is argued that any such program would strain the existing financial resources of the Church, and its existing manpower, the reply should be that we have scarcely begun to weigh the cost of lost opportunities and the sense of failure and frustration which our present chaotic practices entail.

There is much that can be done by way of sociological and psychological analysis to throw light on the perplexities of the ordained ministry and more that can be accomplished by way of the reform and renewal of existing structures.[18] In addition to the parochialism or congregationalism and its innate conservatism, the theologian must call attention to the all-pervasive clericalism which besets the Church at every point in its thinking about ministry and mission. Such clericalism is tellingly revealed in such phrases as "Of course, I'm only a layman," "involving the laity in mission," "using the laity," or "the laity to the help of the clergy." When a man presents himself for ordination, he is commonly spoken of as "entering the Church" or "entering the ministry." [19] What on earth, one wonders, does Holy Baptism signify? The ordained ministry is less than one per cent of the total membership of the Church, as a lay woman, Kathleen Bliss, has pointed out;[20] yet by delegation and default, it is widely assumed that the essential ministry and mission of the Church in the modern world is to be carried out chiefly and, in most cases, exclusively by those who are ordained. Is it any wonder that the Church is largely ineffective in the modern world? Is it any wonder that men deeply committed and devoted break down or retreat into discouragement and defeatism in the face of the tasks they see before them? No one in his right mind could expect the situation to be other than it is.

The very word *ministry* conjures up the image of the *man* who is *ordained* and who is in some sense a full-time *professional* worker in and for the Church.[21] The very existence of such an ordained professional ministry has made it all too easy for the laity, who are 99.5 per cent of the Church, to assume that the real work of the Church is by delegation and default the sole responsibility of such a ministry, an assumption which the clergy themselves have done all too much to perpetuate. Bishop Emrich of Michigan has dubbed such a mentality the "one-man army" view of the ministry, and has urged the Church to explore ways "to take the lid off our manpower." [22] Increasingly, there is a disposition to question whether ministry is exclusively a male prerogative;[23] whether on biblical and historical grounds, let alone pragmatic considerations, it can be maintained that it belongs exclusively to those who are ordained;[24] and whether ordination itself must be thought of as the beginning of a full-time professional career in every instance.

The French worker-priest experiment, with its emphasis upon identification with the working classes and witness through presence and service, has had some influence in

Anglican circles. There are some who see in such a ministry a way of breaking down the all-pervasive clericalism in the Church and the alienation of the proletariat from the institutional church; others, however, question the appropriateness of this particular form of ordained ministry in Britain and North America.[25] A lively discussion has been taking place concerning the possibilities of a "tentmaking ministry" of "part-time" or "nonstipendary priests" who would exercise a sacramental and pastoral ministry while continuing to derive their financial support from some form of "secular" work in the world.[26] With the strong emphasis upon sacramental worship centering in the regular celebration of the Eucharist, many an Anglican feels that lay readers and a perpetual diaconate, that is, deacons who do not anticipate ordination to the priesthood, valuable though their ministries are in the Church, do not suffice to meet the sacramental needs of the Christian community. There are practical difficulties regarding some regular standards of training of a "tentmaking ministry" and the licensing of a man to officiate in a diocese other than that in which he was ordained, to mention only a few. Nevertheless, the case for experimentation, where need and the proper sort of men eager to meet it coincide, is strong, indeed.[27]

Experience in the ecumenical movement is teaching Anglicans that many features of the historic threefold ministry, as it has developed in Britain and overseas, are of secondary importance. For example, it is becoming increasingly clear that although the office of deacon has been maintained, the diaconate, in fact, is little more than a brief period of apprenticeship before an ordinand is advanced to the priesthood. In an era when the Church is everywhere called to realize its vocation as the servant church, the office of deacon needs thorough re-examination. Increasing emphasis is being placed upon the theological, liturgical, and pastoral aspects of the episcopal office and relatively less weight upon the administrative and disciplinary aspects of a bishop's work, at least in popular writing on the subject.[28] Ecumenical encounter is forcing the Anglican Communion to clarify in its own mind as to precisely why it treasures the threefold ministry, and why it must insist upon its maintenance in a reunited Church. It seems likely that the offices of deacon, priest, and bishop are evolving slowly toward forms recognizably continuous with the past, but at the same time very much more flexible and adaptable to the demands which the modern world places upon the ministry of the Church.

The discussions that we have been surveying, stimulating and hopeful though they may be, in themselves reflect a continuing clerical mentality. In Anglican circles, discussion concerning the ministry means, initially at least, discussion of the various possibilities inherent in the ordained ministry. Such discussion raises searching questions about what the Church wants and can reasonably expect from its ordained ministry, and points upon the need for far greater flexibility and professional competence than we are accustomed to. The discussion also points directly to a recovery of the ministry of the whole body of Christians, lay and ordained, which is such an encouraging feature of contemporary thinking about the Church, its ministry and mission. It is to that discussion that we now turn.

Mission and Laos

In both the Old and New Testaments, the word *laos* means "the people," those people of God who have been called into being by the mighty drama of God's self-disclosure of himself recorded in the Old Testament and culminating in the life, ministry, death, and resurrection of Jesus Christ and in the outpouring of the Holy Spirit upon his followers. The people of God are those whose loyalty to the God so disclosed transcends all other loyalties, those people who find the ultimate meaning and purpose of their lives in grateful, joyful, humble obedience to the will and purpose of the God to whom they are called to bear witness and to serve in his world. The ministry and mission of the Church is essentially an extension, a continuation of Jesus Christ's ministry of reconciling man to God. By virtue of their baptism, all Christians are grafted into Christ's Body, the Church, and are called to take their part in the continuing work of ministry. All Christians are called to be ambassadors of reconciliation; each Christian's vocation is, in Luther's phrase, "to be a Christ to his neighbor." All baptized Christians then are laity, that is, members of the *laos,* the people of God. A portion of the *laos,* less than one per cent, is called to an ordained ministry and is commissioned by Christ and the Church to perform particular functions necessary for the well-being of the Body as a whole. They are sometimes referred to as "the other laity." The essential point is that ministry and mission belong to the Church as a whole; all Christians are called to participate in it. It is a disastrous misunderstanding to regard the ordained ministry as the only, or even the chief, form of ministry in the Church, or to regard those who are ordained as those few whose vocation is to be 100 per cent Christian.[29]

A section of the World Council of Churches Assembly at Evanston in 1954 studied "The Laity—the Christian in his Vocation." Their report puts the matter in this way:

Clergy and laity belong together in the Church; if the Church is to perform her mission in the world they need each other. The growing emphasis in many parts of the world upon the function of the laity is not to be understood as an attempt to secure for the laity some larger place or recognition in the Church, nor yet as merely a means to supplement an overburdened and understaffed ordained ministry. It springs from the recovery of the true nature of the Church as the people of God. . . . *The phrase "the ministry of the laity" expresses the privilege of the whole Church to share in Christ's ministry to the world*. We must understand anew the implications of the fact that we are all baptised, that as Christ came to minister, so must all Christians become ministers of His saving purpose according to the particular gift of the Spirit which each has received, as messengers of the hope revealed in Christ.[30]

"The privilege of the whole Church to share in Christ's ministry to the world," that is the insight which offers hope for breaking down the clericalism of the Church. The ministry and mission of the Church belong to the body as a whole. The Church is that social organism which exists for the sake of those who are not its members. It is called to the grateful obedient service of God's world. The forms and opportunities for that service and witness are as rich and varied as are the manifold talents and needs of human beings. Jesus provided in concrete terms some idea of what is involved in his parable of the sheep and the goats (Matt. 25:31-46). The purpose of the parable is not to provide information about a last judgment or to stimulate speculation about it. Jesus was primarily concerned in this parable with the quality of life manifested by his disciples here and now in this world. The crux of the parable lies in the familiar words, "Inasmuch as ye did it unto one of these my brethren, even the least, ye did it unto me." The ministry and mission of the Christian is to give food to the hungry, drink to the thirsty, to visit the sick and those in prison, to do whatever love requires in the specific situation in which one finds himself. This is not to be seen primarily as an obligation but as a privilege, as the Evanston report makes clear. Jesus knew well what his followers have so often forgotten, that faith, hope, and love are never permanent possessions. If one is to partake of them, they must be shared. It is in the giving of them to others that one participates more fully in them himself.

At several points, we have commented on the temptation to self-concern and self-preoccupation on the part of the

Church. In the context of the ministry of the laity, the Evanston Assembly had this to say:

The real battles of faith today are being fought in factories, shops, offices, and farms, in political parties and government agencies, in countless homes, in the press, radio and television, in the relationship of nations. Very often it is said that the Church should "go into these spheres," but the fact is that the Church *is* already in these spheres in the persons of its laity.[31]

The ordained ministry cannot and ought not be present in all these spheres of life all the time. Moreover, they cannot and ought not expect that they will have the professional competence to deal with the complex problems which arise as Christians wrestle with the often-conflicting obligations of their various responsibilities to God, their families, their employers, their particular fields of work, and their integrity as human beings. It seems abundantly clear that if the Church is to fulfill its calling in and for the world, the ministry of the future must be one in which those not ordained will play a far greater part. The clergy cannot undertake the mission of the Church to the world by themselves. They can and must equip the whole Church for its mission. Increasingly, it appears that the role of the clergy will be seen as that of serving the health of the laity. Initially, this might appear to some clergy to lower the ideal and role of the ordained ministry, but, in fact, nothing could be further from the truth. The higher one's view of the role and function of the laity, the higher one's view of the clergy, whose role it is to serve the health of the Church as a whole.[32]

Commenting further on the Evanston report and Jesus' words, "Ye are the salt of the earth," the Central Committee of the World Council of Churches published the following statement:

The salt fulfills its function only, after having been assembled and cleansed, it is scattered again to be dissolved. Likewise the

Church lives by a process of assembling and scattering. It is brought together from all peoples, occupations and groups for worship and for recognizable "organized activities." It is scattered as its members, and predominantly its lay members, disperse themselves in the life of the world. As salt fulfills its function only when scattered and dissolved, so an indispensable part of the ministry of the Church is exercised when the Church is in its scattered phase. This process of withdrawal and return, of being assembled and being scattered, is not accidental but essential to the Church's life.[33]

It is a disastrous misunderstanding of the Church's life if one's vision is confined to the Church as *ekklesia,* that is, the Church as it gathers or assembles for worship and for recognizable "organized activities." This aspect of the Church's life is essential for its health and well-being. Christians require the inspiration, study, mutual support, and encouragement that the Church gathered affords. Common worship is an activity offered to the glory of God and ought never be regarded merely as a means to some further end. But it is equally the case that our lives test the sincerity of our worship. The Church can no more live exclusively in its gathered aspect than can the human being breathe simply by inhaling. The Church's life is a rhythm of gathering and dispersing. The Church is *diaspora* as well as *ekklesia.* Witness and service of one's neighbor in the world is as much a part of the Church's life as is eucharistic worship, preaching, and Bible study. The nature of the Church as *diaspora* cries out for recognition today—the demands that *diaspora* places upon Christians, the joys and opportunities it affords, the implications of this for the Church when it gathers, and the role it implies for the clergy.

The ministry of the laity must not be seen as just one more clerical scheme to breathe life and vitality into the institutional church and its activities when it gathers. It is not a device to get more people to do more jobs around the church building or parish house. Rather, it implies an entire reorientation in the thinking and relationships between laity and clergy. The reorientation will be slow in coming and must involve the giving up of many a cherished assumption. To date, most of what has been written on the subject has been written by clergy. There is an urgent need to listen to lay men and women as to what they seek and expect from the Church, and how, in concrete and practical terms, they understand their mission and ministry. It seems likely that the equipping and training an awakened laity will demand is beyond the competence of many a parish priest whose entire ministry has been dominated by the unexamined assumptions implicit in clericalism. The best resources of the Church on a regional basis will be required. It also seems likely that an awakened laity will underline the scandal of a divided Church and supply a new impetus toward the reunion of the churches. Many a layman concerned about exercising a significant ministry of witness and service feels isolated enough without wishing to limit his opportunities for mutual concern, encouragement, and support to members of his own particular branch of the Christian Church.

A Lay Theology

One result of the clericalism which has afflicted the Church has been that the discipline of theology itself has come to be regarded as almost exclusively the preserve of the professional and clerical theologian. To a regrettable extent, theologians have been content to write for one another and for a broader clerical audience. Not surprisingly, the very word "theology" has become synonomous with the otherworldly, the esoteric, and the obscure. Some years ago, Alec R. Vidler wrote in a pessimistic vein about the future of a clerical, or academic, theology and suggested that the future of the discipline lay in the emergence of a genuinely lay-oriented theology.[34] More recently, J. A. T. Robinson has sketched in the broadest of outlines what such a lay theology might imply. Dr. Robinson does not have in mind an amateurish theology, nor one in the narrow sense of a theology for those who are not clergy. Lay theology "is a theology which is impelled by the needs of the *laos,* or whole people of God, to *be* the Church *in* the world. Just as in the past, it has been the councils of the Church, the monasteries, the universities, the training seminaries, that have been the springs from which new theological thinking has been fed into the Church, so tomorrow I would expect its creative source to be the engagement of the *laos* in the life of the world." [35] The forms and structures within which such a theology might emerge are scarcely visible as yet, although the lay academies and ecumenical centers may be an indication of where to look, Dr. Robinson suggests.

It is worthy of comment that the last three decades have seen the quiet and unself-conscious witness of an impressive group of "lay theologians" in various disciplines. I have in mind such persons as T. S. Eliot, Charles Williams, C. S. Lewis, Dorothy Sayers, and, more recently, D. L. Munby, John Lawrence, John Wren-Lewis, William Stringfellow, Monica Furlong, Marianne Micks, and A. Denis Baly. They exhibit diverse interests and clearly form no school of thought. At the same time, their emergence and contributions are noteworthy. Only a few general observations about their work will be made here—a fact which may betray the unconscious clericalism and professionalism of the present writer!

It happens that each of the persons mentioned is an accomplished writer, and for this reason, their contributions have come to the attention of the reading public. Each exhibits a high degree of professional competence in his or her chosen discipline, whether it be the writing of poetry, literary criticism, novels or detective stories, journalism, the law, economics, or the geography of the Middle East. Such persons command the attention of the reading public because they combine a high degree of professional competence, which has won the respect of their colleagues, with fresh and penetrating insight into the meaning of the Christian faith in the modern world. Invariably, their professional work shapes and illuminates their understanding of Christian faith.[36] Often, as is the case with C. S. Lewis or Dorothy Sayers, it provides fruitful analogies rather different from those which naturally occur to the professional theologian or philosopher.[37] Because they have no vested interest in the existing structures of the institutional church as it presently exists, some of the contributions, notably those of John Wren-Lewis, D. L. Munby, and Monica Furlong, are unusually astringent and pointed in their criticisms of the status quo.[38] The writing of T. S. Eliot and C. S. Lewis is rather more appreciative of the heritage of the past, and is concerned with interpretation and illumination of familiar symbols and forms rather than their replacement. On the whole, the lay theologians have addressed and reached a far wider audience than all but a few of the academic and professional theologians. Their very skill as writers has made them unusually effective in the communication of what they wished to convey. Theirs is a distinctly lay, rather than clerical, witness and spirituality, as, for example, in a play like Eliot's *Cocktail Party*. The concerns and the language are those of persons very much a part of this world—secular, in other words. The very emergence of such a number of lay theologians in the middle decades of the present century speaks for the continuing vitality of the Christian tradition, despite its many failures. The contributions illustrate the necessity of broadening the scope of theology to take account of the interests and work of other than professional theologians. It would be hazardous in the extreme to predict the extent to which the theology of the future will become a genuinely lay theology in the sense of being a theology relevant to the needs and concerns of an awakened *laos*. One can only point to encouraging signs on the horizon and hope that they will multiply and be given every encouragement.

CHAPTER 7

The Current Ferment

THE year 1963 will go down in the annals of English religious thought as the year of *Honest to God*. Occasionally, it happens that an event or a book will both capture the public imagination and at the same time dramatize and focus developments which have for some time been stirring beneath the surface of public attention. Clearly, such an event was the publication in March, 1963, of a slim paperback by John A. T. Robinson, Bishop of Woolwich. A book which its author and publisher expected might eventually sell seven to ten thousand copies rapidly became an international best seller. Currently, there are more than half a million copies in print, and the book is being translated into at least seven foreign languages. In the nine months following its release, *Honest to God* "appears to have sold more rapidly than any new book of serious theology in the history of the world." [1]

Commentary on the book in the popular as well as the church press reached flood-tide proportions in the months following its publication. A selection of reviews, letters received by the author or publisher, together with several more lengthy essays, was published in December of 1963 by the SCM Press under the title *The Honest to God Debate*. Numerous pamphlets and paperbacks discussing the controversial book have appeared in the last eighteen months, and discussions of the ideas raised by Dr. Robinson's book have appeared in most theological journals of importance.[2] Discussion of the ideas presented by the book will be made in several subsequent chapters. Just now, my concern lies in the impact of the book itself and in what its astonishing reception discloses about the religious situation in England and elsewhere in the English-speaking world.

The Impact of Honest to God

How is one to account for the remarkable sales of a book on a religious subject? The book was released in paperback form, which made it readily available at a nominal sum. Once a book becomes a best seller, that very fact stimulates further sales. More significant are certain characteristics of the British scene. To an extent unknown in the United States, England has a national press and national television. An interview on television or an article in one of the major newspapers is immediately carried to a large audience throughout the country. Ideas, even theological ideas, can be disseminated almost instantaneously. Excerpts from the book appeared in a national newspaper, *The Observer,* of March 17, 1963, under the head, "Our Image of God Must Go," along with a picture of the Bishop of Woolwich in full ecclesiastical attire. Undoubtedly, that article launched the run-away sales. The book was written by a bishop, and when a bishop speaks on any subject, particularly a controversial one, his voice is still listened to in England. Here was a man holding high office in the Church who dared to write freely and openly of some of his wrestlings with doubt and uncertainty. When a bishop speaks his mind frankly, says something other than the time-worn clichés and sounds somewhat heterodox, even the non-Christian finds his interest titillated. Is the bishop a heretic? Will he be rebuked by higher authority? Will he be forced to resign or perhaps even be deposed? Since being consecrated Bishop of Woolwich in 1959, John Robinson had gained considerable notoriety and a rebuke from Archbishop Geoffrey Fisher when he and Fr. Martin Jarrett-Kerr of the Community of the Resurrection testified in court supporting D. H. Lawrence's *Lady Chatterley's Lover* against charges of obscenity.

Hence, the bishop was well known to the public. His doings and statements are good copy for the popular press.

Honest to God was written in a relatively brief period of enforced leisure while its author recuperated from an illness. Dr. Robinson wrote "in a tentative and exploratory way," and the book was not consciously directed to the large popular audience that has comprised the bulk of its readers.[3] Critics have been quick to point out that neither the argument nor the language is altogether clear in many places. Given more leisure, the author would undoubtedly have removed obscurities and confusions, written a more balanced and judicious exposition of his position, that is, written a different book. The very speed with which the book was written gives it an intensity, an emotional power, that a more scholarly and balanced treatment might not have had. One suspects that Dr. Robinson, himself, was surprised by the emotional impact of his book and the passionate response, pro and con, which it has evoked. The book comes from the depths of the man; it is an outpouring of ideas long held in the recesses of his mind. Its power, in part, lies in its ability to speak to those partially conscious stirrings and perplexities deep in the minds and hearts of many of its readers.

In Britain and elsewhere, one is conscious of a significant, if as yet largely inarticulate, lay group, partially inside and partially outside the Church, for whom theological ideas continue to have meaning. These individuals appear to find many of the traditional patterns of parochial organizational life trivial. They are distinguished by their wholehearted acceptance of modern science and technology. They are unmistakably children of the present century. They are likely to find much of the language and thought forms in which Christianity has been expressed meaningless. Not interested or moved by evangelism in any traditional sense, they are inclined to regard the essence of Christianity as service to others. They are themselves deeply involved in work "in the world." They long for an interpretation of Christian faith and practice which will give meaning and depth to the conflicts they engage in day by day. Many of them have turned away from the institutional church because they no longer find the traditional "answers" helpful. Some continue nominal membership in the Church but find centers of meaning and opportunities for service outside its institutional life. Between the core of active, committed Christians in Britain and, at the opposite end of the spectrum, the conscious and articulate atheists and agnostics, there remains a large ill-defined group, possibly as much as eighty per cent of the population, who are slowly drifting away from the institutional church. There remain many on the fringe or outside the Church who are not utterly indifferent, who continue to hope wistfully and sometimes despairingly for a faith to live by. By and large, *Honest to God* has made its impression upon this large ill-defined group. Dr. Robinson seems to have found the range, if sales and his mailbag are any indication. Certain of the ideas discussed are those which have been put aside in the form of unanswered questions by people inside and outside the Church. Many a matter half-consciously suppressed or left smoldering in the recesses of the mind has been dragged into the light of open discussion. Of those who have been so bold as to speak positively of the book, the dominant note has been one of relief and liberation: what the editor of *Prism* described as "the almost audible gasp of relief . . . when these things are at last being said openly." [4] Many discouraged people, numb with repeated disappointment, felt that at long last here was a bishop trying to speak to their perplexities and uncertainties. *Honest to God* was in one sense a missionary tract written by a man who knew and understood many of the questions addressed to the Church by the "outsider" as a result of his years as dean of a Cambridge college and more recently as a suffragan bishop in South London, where there has been over the years a ruinous falling away from the Church as an institution. The book comes from one of the frontiers. Its author says of it: "Its whole argument depends on the fact that I am trying to help those who are on the fringe of the faith or quite outside it. This concern determines almost every line of what I wrote." [5]

Reaction in the Church of England has been decidedly mixed. The conservative *Church Times* complained: "It is not every day that a bishop goes on public record as apparently denying almost every Christian doctrine of the Church in which he holds office." [6] The Bishop of Pontefract quoted one of his clergy as saying: "We feel that the ground is being cut from under our feet." Describing a widespread clerical reaction, the bishop continued: "As they slave away at their sick visiting, in Sunday schools, taking their confirmation classes, running their clubs and organizations, preparing their sermons —and the rest—they have the feeling that the foundations are being eaten away. Things which they have held to faithfully all their lives are being questioned; things that they have done with devotion all the years of their ministry are dismissed as obsolete, unnecessary, and ill conceived." [7] Many a clergyman attacked the Bishop of Woolwich and his book in parish bulletins or papers, thus swelling the sales further. The *Church of England Newspaper* observed, however, that a reading of *Honest to God* "should be accompanied by a recollection of the conspicuous failure of the Church of England as a whole to make Christianity meaningful to this generation." [8]

Initially, much of the uproar within the Church turned on a question of ecclesiastical taste. Had the bishop misbehaved? If so, ought he be punished? Three questions emerged in the public discussion: Should excerpts of the book have been published in a national newspaper? Should a bishop allow himself to write a book which might cause distress among faithful Churchmen? Should such a book have been published by anyone holding office in the Church? In his presidential address to the Convocation of Canterbury, May 6, 1963, Archbishop Ramsey referred at some length to *Honest to God* and to the article which preceded it:

I was specially grieved at the method chosen by the bishop for presenting his ideas to the public. We are asked to think that the enterprise was a matter of being "tentative," "thinking aloud," "raising questions," and the like. But the initial method chosen was a newspaper article, crystal clear in its argument, and provocative in its shape and statement, to tell the public that the concept of a personal God as held in popular Christianity and in orthodox doctrine is outmoded, and that atheists and agnostics are right to reject it. . . . Of course the association of this thesis with a bishop of the Church caused the public sensation and did much damage. Many of us who read the article and its slogans might not have had the opportunity or the necessary brains for reading the book referred to; and the message which the bishop succeeded in disseminating in the country was the negative one I have described.

With reference to the first question—Should excerpts from the book have been published in a national newspaper?—the Archbishop's position has been widely applauded in the Church. To be sure, the ideas expressed in the book were new to the general public. *The Observer,* on the other hand, could not refrain from asking whether the Archbishop objected to clarity and provocative statements from his clergy. The hard fact stands, however, that the ideas of the book could not be set forth adequately in an article which did, in fact, cause wide distress in the Church, not least among its clergy.[9] At the same time, it was the article which introduced the book to those outside the Church, and thus made possible the wide circulation it has since enjoyed. There is an implied contempt for the laity in the position that only clergy should discuss the sort of issues raised by Dr. Robinson.

Should a bishop have published a book that might cause distress among the faithful? The Archbishop took pains to affirm the responsibility of any bishop not to cause needless offense. In the Preface of his book, the Bishop of Woolwich acknowledges in unmistakable terms his sense of responsibility to uphold the faith. The question remains somewhat cloudy. A conflict of responsibilities may arise if a bishop in defending the faith, as he understands it, does, in fact, cause distress among the faithful. The Bishop of Woolwich is prepared to afflict the comfortable upon occasion and has been censured by two Archbishops for doing so. Not all agree with them, however. A Cambridge dean wrote to *The Times:* "One cannot but admire the sense of responsibility shown by the episcopal bench as a whole. It is so profound that it has prevented them from saying anything of theological importance for at least the past two decades. A generation has grown up who know William Temple only as a name and who have never heard of Charles Gore, Hensley Henson, and William Barnes. Hence the shock of young people when a bishop publishes anything they can think and argue about." [10]

Should a book such as *Honest to God* have been published by anyone holding office in the Church? The answer here seems to be a clear affirmative. Some ten days before his address in Convocation, the Archbishop of Canterbury published a small pamphlet, "Image Old and New," discussing the theological issues raised by the book. In his address, he reaffirmed his view "that the questions discussed in it are real questions, and the effort to open up new modes of contact between our faith and a secular age is one with which I feel much sympathy." [11] A lay comment on this aspect of the controversy is particularly interesting.

Religious violence is at the moment out of fashion, but there are plenty of people in all the churches (and a little curiously, some outside them) who feel that religion must only be discussed with the brakes full on, since the pursuit of truth is fraught with such unspeakable perils. . . . What, one wonders, are they so afraid of? That the new theologians will not come up with the old answers in the back of the book? But then, as Gamaliel said, why worry? If their counsel be of men, they will soon make fools of themselves. And if their counsel be of God, then we had better think twice before taking Him on as an opponent. . . . But we can perhaps go further than Gamaliel and say that, whatever the outcome of their thinking, they are doing their fellow Christians a service by producing the tension, the "no" to their "yes," which makes fruitful dialectics possible. As many of us often discover in ourselves it is by living with our tensions, by holding two contradictory and conflicting ideas together within us for a period, that we achieve self-knowledge and a genuine peace of mind. And one of the impressive things about the new Christian radicals is the marks of the conflict going on within them, which compels them to attempt to identify themselves with agnostics, as St. Francis tried to identify with beggars, say, or St. Vincent de Paul to impersonate a galley-slave.[12]

In spite of the storm of controversy touched off by *Honest to God* and the bitter opposition the book provoked in certain quarters, the freedom of a clergyman, even a bishop, to publish a book containing controversial ideas has not been effectively challenged by responsible authority in the Church.

Robinson's Central Argument

John Robinson is very much a child of the established Church of England. His father and grandfather were canons of Canterbury, and he was reared in the Cathedral precincts. He says that he has never seriously questioned his vocation to the ordained ministry of the Church. Throughout his writings, one finds evidence of a deep and vigorous Christian commitment. At the same time, he is also a child of the present century, his life and mind shaped and molded by its culture and characteristic thought forms. *Honest to God* is "a dialogue between religious man and secular man. And secular man is just as much inside the Church as out of it, and just as much inside myself. Indeed, my book was born of the fact that I knew myself a man committed without reservation to Christ *and* a man committed, without possibility of return to modern twentieth-century secular society. It was written out of the belief that both of these convictions must be taken with equal seriousness and that they *cannot* be incompatible." [13]

The tension between traditional Christian faith and twentieth-century secularist assumptions arises for Dr. Robinson in three crucial areas: (1) the reality and presence of God in a world understood in secular terms; (2) the distinctive character and properties of "religious" language, that is, the traditional language of the Bible and of Christian worship; and (3) what it means to be a Christian in a largely indifferent, if not hostile, secular society. A brief discussion of these three central issues serves to indicate the theological, as distinguished from the popular, significance of Dr. Robinson's book.

Who is God? How can man come to know him? Where and how is divine activity in the world to be perceived and understood? Is there any God to whom modern secular man can turn in faith and worship? As Bonhoeffer has written, "Man has learned to cope with all questions of importance without recourse to God as a working hypothesis. . . . As in the scientific field, so in human affairs generally, what we call 'God' is being more and more edged out of life, losing more and more ground." [14] Dr. Robinson is sharply critical of popular theism of the last hundred years or more. God is not to be understood as *a being* beside other beings, whose existence can be proven or at least argued about. Neither is God *a person,* albeit a super person. God's activity in the world is not to be traced in the "gaps" of present scientific knowledge, nor can we literally picture God as someone located "up there" or even "out there" in space. There are not two worlds, one the familiar world of nature, man, and history, and another world, realm, or sphere of supranature in which God and spiritual beings reign supreme and which "perforates" the world of everyday experience. There is only one world, and if God is to be known

and worshiped, it will be in the familiar world of human experience and not in some shadowy realm beside, above, or
beyond the world we already experience. The dilemma seems
to be either an antiquated supranaturalism which seems tied
to a prescientific world picture, or an atheistic or agnostic
naturalism, with or without religious overtones. Following
Paul Tillich and Dietrich Bonhoeffer, Dr. Robinson seeks to
go beyond the dilemma by urging a recovery of the presence
and otherness or transcendence of God in, through, and beneath the realities of everyday human experience. The place to
seek God is in the midst of life, in its depths, and not in some
realm apart from human experience. The God who seemingly
has vanished from a world understood in secular terms is to
be rediscovered as the creative source and ground of all that
is when *this world* is plumbed in its depths. God is to be found
not on the boundaries of human knowledge, but in the midst
of life, at the heart of nature and of human relationships, if
we will have eyes to see and ears to hear. The practical implications of this turning to the world is brilliantly illustrated
in *Honest to God* in the chapter dealing with prayer, which
especially has the ring of authenticity since it was written out
of deep personal experience. Had he wished to, Dr. Robinson
might have supported his position by numerous references to
the Hebrew prophets and psalmists. His thought, on the positive side, is surely congruous with the central affirmation of
Christian faith that God reveals himself most fully to men in
and through the life of the man Jesus of Nazareth, so that in
him the Christian affirms that "God was in Christ, reconciling
the world unto himself." The line of thought here advocated
is congruous also with the sacramental principle that in,
through, and under consecrated bread and wine the presence
of the living Christ is given to the worshiper. The line of
thought proposed by Dr. Robinson is one suggested by the
writings of Paul Tillich, Dietrich Bonhoeffer, Rudolf Bultmann, and Martin Buber. In spite of the many differences be-

tween these diverse thinkers, each one decisively points to this world as the place where God is to be found for twentieth-century man, by whatever name God may be called.

Initially, this may appear to be atheism in that the god of the popular theism of the last several centuries has been decisively dethroned. Thus, Antony Flew, writing in *The Observer,* is critical of the use that Dr. Robinson makes of Paul Tillich. "Does Dr. Robinson appreciate that it must make Tillich's theology, in all but Tillich's own peculiar sense, atheistic?" [15] The same criticism is made by Alasdair Mac-Intyre, who charges that Dr. Robinson uses "religious language to mask an atheistic vacuum." For Professor MacIntyre, "what is striking about Dr. Robinson's book is first and foremost that he is an atheist." [16] It is Professor MacIntyre's thesis that contemporary theology faces a hopeless dilemma. It can continue to use the traditional thought forms, thus remaining clearly and obviously faithful to its roots in the Bible and the classical Christian tradition. To do so, however, is to be doomed to speak to a steadily shrinking group of those who have already accepted the Christian message. The alternative is to seek to address the world outside the Church in its own terms. This involves recasting the Christian message in thought forms understandable by modern secular man. As soon as this is done, however, the gospel is diluted and adulterated. One has begun the slippery descent into atheism or agnosticism. Professor MacIntyre believes that this is the fundamental failure of the theologies of Tillich, Bultmann, and Bonhoeffer. Much of the religious language remains, but it has been transposed into a secular key in such a way that it points decisively away from classical Christianity.

Antony Flew and Alasdair MacIntyre are knowledgeable, if astringent, critics. As they and others have shown, it is not difficult to attack philosophically the popular theism of the nineteenth and twentieth centuries. Theology has much to learn from their criticism, along with their insistence on consistency and logical precision in the use of words. It is possible to argue, as Professor MacIntyre does, that the theology of Tillich, Bultmann, and Bonhoeffer in fact points away from the popular theism that they find inadequate. It is premature to leap to the conclusion that they are therefore essentially atheistic, however. The intention of these theologians is to recover an understanding of God very much broader and deeper than the doctrinal expressions of the last several centuries. Whether such an exercise can be carried through to a successful conclusion remains to be seen. It is scarcely a task to be expected of a decade, let alone of a particular theologian or a single book. Dr. Robinson concludes his brief reply to Professor MacIntyre, "I decline to accept as Mr. MacIntyre states it, 'the harsh dilemma of a would-be contemporary theology,' of either addressing an 'in-group' or accepting the atheism of its hearers. I believe the response to my book has shown that a third alternative is very much a live option." [17] Dr. Robinson will not allow that, in rejecting the popular theism which he sometimes caricatures in the early chapters of his book, he has capitulated to atheism.

In a book of 140 pages, one does not expect to find a fully developed theology of God. There are a number of ambiguities and unresolved problems in this area. Dr. Robinson's treatment has certain affinities, undoubtedly unconscious, with the theologies of immanence associated with J. R. Illingworth and R. J. Campbell in the first decade of this century, [18] and with J. F. Bethune-Baker because of his thesis of emergent evolution. Not surprisingly, Dr. Robinson felt the need to anticipate and refute in advance the charge of pantheism. What is needed is a much clearer and fuller account of the transcendence encountered in God's immanence and the immanence of the transcendent One there encountered, to borrow William Temple's formula. [19] Any such treatment must be developed without Temple's philosophical idealism, however, if it is to speak to men in the nineteen sixties and thereafter. In *Honest to God,* there is a dichotomy between the opening chapters, in which the objections to any language of transcendence are apparently conceded, thus leaving one with a God entirely "down there," and the later chapters, in which a good deal of traditional language is unconsciously reintroduced as apparently meaningful. The dichotomy undoubtedly exists in Dr. Robinson's own mind, but he can scarcely expect to give away his cake and, then, eat it later. The significance of Dr. Robinson's treatment of God lies in his firm grasp of the crucial problem for contemporary theology, his awareness of what is at stake, and his somewhat tentative suggestions for next steps toward a more adequate and comprehensive solution. His book neither sought nor achieved that solution within its brief compass.

Much the same assessment can be made of the discussion of the nature and function of religious language and the question of what it means to be a Christian in a secular society. Fuller discussion of these issues must await later chapters. At this juncture, it suffices to note that each problem is a crucial one, the first for faith and the second for practice. In dealing with the former question, Dr. Robinson's point of departure is the proposal of Rudolf Bultmann to "demythologize" the Bible, that is, free the essential message from its clothing in a mythical and prescientific world view. The second issue, that of the calling of a Christian in secular society, is opened up by Dietrich Bonhoeffer's fragmentary suggestions for a "religionless Christianity" in a world "come of age," that is, a world no longer dependent upon theism and the God hypothesis.

It is easy to overestimate Dr. Robinson's indebtedness to Paul Tillich, Bultmann, and Bonhoeffer. He is careful to dissociate himself from Tillich's systematic theology as a whole.[20] He has no desire to be drawn into the later stages of the Bultmann controversy.[21] Several critics have questioned the depth of his understanding of Bonhoeffer, particularly the latter's use of the word *religionlos.*[22] What Dr. Robinson sought and found in each of these theologians were certain seminal ideas. His originality lies in the juxtaposition and powerful expression he was able to give to these ideas for a public largely ignorant of them. Although *Honest to God* seemed at first a revolutionary book, its author noted in his preface, "The one thing of which I am fairly sure is that, in retrospect, it will be seen to have erred in not being nearly radical enough." [23] Dr. Robinson describes himself: "I have been, and I remain, primarily a Biblical theologian and a fairly conservative one at that. I have no desire to 'preach any other gospel,' nor do I wish to deny anything in the faith which the creeds enshrine. My sole concern and contention is for the Scriptural revelation of God as dynamic personal love." [24] His own estimate of the character of his book, his theological intention, and the description of himself in the context of contemporary theological discussion strikes this writer as very much sounder and more accurate than the judgments of most of his critics to date.

Forerunners of Honest to God

Honest to God cannot be understood and appreciated if it is seen as an isolated phenomenon. It is a symptom and expression of a situation of ferment very much broader and deeper than the casual reader is likely to assume. That ferment has been brewing for some time beneath the apparently tranquil surface of Anglican theology. Just now my purpose is to note other books and theologians whose work illustrates many of the same concerns and ideas that have moved John Robinson. What is interesting and, perhaps, surprising is that a great deal of the work has been carried on with little awareness that others were mining the same lode. It happened that a fair amount of work "broke surface" and was published in the space of twelve months during 1962–63. These books and those of a similar nature which preceded them were neither caused nor occasioned by *Honest to God*. They, together with it, belong to a larger phenomenon.

In retrospect, the first hints of a possible new ferment in British theology are to be seen in a slim volume by Ronald Gregor Smith, *The New Man* (1956). The most interesting and suggestive chapters are the two concluding ones, in which Smith calls for "this-worldly Transcendence" and draws heavily on the thought of Bonhoeffer, Tillich, and Martin Buber. Gregor Smith's intention is to help his readers to recover a sense of the divine mystery in the events, concerns, and relationships of this world. The treatment is positive and constructive. It is also somewhat academic, and the book attracted relatively little attention when it appeared.

In 1957, E. R. Wickham's *Church and People in an Industrial City* carefully documented the decline in influence and effectiveness of the Church of England among the middle and working classes. The focus of the study was the city of Sheffield, where Wickham had been engaged in a pioneering industrial mission for more than a decade. What was true in Sheffield is true elsewhere in England, and the picture of a ruinous decline in effectiveness of the Church over the years alerted some, at least, to the dire situation that faced the Church if it insisted on simply doing the same things in the same old way. That same year, Alec R. Vidler published *Essays in Liberality*. Safely academic and apparently occasional as the essays seemed to be at the time, their significance is very much clearer in the light of events during 1963. Of particular importance is the opening essay, in which Dr. Vidler carefully distinguishes liberality from liberalism, whether political or theological, and calls for a revival of the liberal spirit in theology. The realism of the essay "The Future of Theology" helps one understand the background of the recent ferment. Dr. Vidler was no more encouraging about the state of academic theology than was Wickham about the effectiveness of the Church in the industrial Midlands. "Worldly Holiness" has become almost a cliché since *Honest to God*. Those put off by the term should turn to Vidler's essay "Holy Worldliness." Not least of the virtues of Dr. Vidler's careful treatment is his clear statement of that worldliness which is *not* Christian. The point of the essay is essentially that of Chapter V in *Honest to God*. What the essay may lack in emotional power, it more than compensates for by its clarity, sanity, and balance.

The year 1958 saw a meeting of the Lambeth Conference. That provided the occasion for several composite volumes of essays, a favorite literary form for Anglican theologians. In the United States, the volume was *Viewpoints,* edited by John Coburn and W. Norman Pittenger. Particularly interesting in the light of subsequent events are the essays by Emma Lou Benignus, Charles R. Stinnette, Jr., and William H. Poteat. Miss Benignus calls for a recovery of the place and mission of the laity. Charles Stinnette illustrates the fruitful insights to be discovered for theology from depth psychology, and William Poteat has some hard things to say about American popular religion as it is found in the American Episcopal Church. In England, the comparable volume was *Essays in Anglican Self-Criticism,* edited by David M. Paton. The *Times Literary Supplement* observed that "whatever else may be said against the Church of England no one could suggest that there is any other association of men which criticizes itself more strenuously." The contributors were for the most part younger men, definitely not part of the ecclesiastical "establishment." They went about their task with great gusto and effectiveness. William Nicholls, drawing on Bonhoeffer, Bultmann, and Tillich, as well as Karl Barth, scores the Church for its lack of concern with theology as a "critical science." D. L. Munby catalogues the demise of "Christian sociology" and the neglect of economics and sociology alike in the Church under the heading "The Lack of Technical Competence." Another layman, John Wren-Lewis, is sharply critical of recent attempts at apologetics in his essay "Integrity in Apologetics: or the Dangers of Resorting to Bluff in Theology." The volume as a whole is larded with keen observations, astringent criticism, and repays the careful reader. Not one of the above-mentioned books created much of a stir when it first appeared. Taken together, they are indicative of a discontent with things as they are, an impatience with the old ways, ecclesiastical and theological, and an awareness that, without some radical thinking and action, the future of the Church is bleak indeed. They are a portent of things to come.

It was during the winter of 1962-63 that the ferment clearly "broke surface." In November, a group of Cambridge scholars published a volume of essays entitled *Soundings*.[25] According to its editor, Alec R. Vidler, *Soundings* consciously sees itself as following in the tradition of earlier composite volumes, in tone and purpose closest to *Essays and Reviews* (1860) and *Foundations* (1911). The contributors to *Soundings* are a diverse group and represent none of the traditional parties in the Church of England. The contributors have in common the conviction that there are important and difficult intellectual problems that the Church has neglected or failed to face in sufficient depth in recent years. To their minds, these questions are steadily becoming more urgent and are likely to remain with us for a long time since they do not lend themselves to easy or facile answers. Moreover, they are doubtful how long vitality in church life and worship can survive a continuing neglect of the basic issues of a systematic and apologetic theology. Under the inspiration and leadership of Alec R. Vidler, *Soundings* is a deliberate attempt to rouse Anglican theology from its dogmatic slumbers. The predominant tone of the volume is cautious, indeed skeptical, about the very possibility of conclusive theological "answers" at this juncture. As Hugh Montefiore puts it, "There are times when Christian theology, if it is true to itself, must be silent; and this may be one of them. It is a time of agonizing strain and testing for those who search for coherence and meaning. And if the darkness lasts too long the Church's intellectuals may lose heart and her enemies rejoice." [26] Nevertheless, if theology is to

move forward, the problems must be stated and faced. Therefore, Montefiore continues in Keats's words, "I leaped head-
long into the sea and thereby have become better acquainted
with the soundings, the quicksands and the rocks, than if I
had stayed upon the green shore, and piped a silly pipe, and
took tea and comfortable advice." [27]

Soundings, then, is a book for the serious reader, prepared
to take a long hard look at the quicksands and rocks. Aware of
some of them, the sensitive reader will suspect that others are
lurking beneath the surface and that the ship must carefully pick
its way through them if it is to do something other than rot at
anchor. The book says little about the issues that have held
the center of attention in the Church since World War II.
There is no essay in biblical theology, none on liturgical renewal, and nothing about the ecumenical movement. There is
no tea or comfortable advice. The tone is sober and chastened.
The book turns to a set of problems generally neglected in the
last several decades. Its very incompleteness and failure to
deal with these problems in a serene and confident manner in-
vites theology to take a new direction as it attempts to make up
the deficiencies evident in *Soundings* itself. In effect, the
volume as a whole says, "Look here, these are the issues that
a serious theology should be concerned with. We see a good
many more problems than answers. The one thing we are confident of is that we know the sort of questions theology should
be concerned with in the next decade or more. If you don't
care for our solutions, such as they are, try your hand at
better ones. But take care not to neglect the difficulties we've
pointed out. The questions are too important for the thin and
complacent diet to which we've become accustomed." The
book raises some of the questions the "outsider" might address
to the Church if he thought there was anyone about who would
take them seriously.

What are the issues to which *Soundings* directs our attention? Howard E. Root, in an essay titled "Beginning All Over

Again," points out the lack of a solidly based natural theology, regrets that neither theology nor philosophy seems unduly disturbed by its absence, and concludes that we have been asking the wrong sort of questions; for example, "proofs for the existence of God." There is an uneasy truce between science and religion, John S. Habgood tells us. This has made it possible for the sciences and theology to go about their respective tasks while largely ignoring the other. As a long-range solution, division of territory and truce is no more adequate now than it was when Aubrey Moore criticized it in *Lux Mundi* seventy-five years ago. G. F. Woods is concerned about the ambiguities in commonly used theological terms and thinks that the methods of linguistic analysis will throw some light on our confusions. He provides an illustrative sample in his examination of the word "transcendent." H. A. Williams applies Freudian insights to illuminate the question of morality and the seven root, or capital, sins. Because he notes in passing that extramarital sexual intercourse may have redemptive as well as destructive possibilities, this essay provoked the most initial comment and likely enough ensured the wide distribution of the book. The relative isolation of Western Christianity is no longer possible, Ninian Smart believes. He would have us take account of the challenges implicit in other religions. Granted the importance of sacred scripture, which scriptures should we turn to as authoritative, and why? Can we maintain that revelation of a personal God given in history carries a unique claim upon the allegiance of thinking men whose history and culture has not led them to place the same value on the categories of the personal and the historical that seems natural to Western man? Biblical criticism, another paper observes, has dealt a mortal blow to older theories of the inspiration and authority of the Bible. Do we have left a really adequate view of the authority of the New Testament? The late J. N. Sanders surveys the possible answers and finds the results inconclusive. What of Christology? Are the formulas of

Chalcedon adequate, let alone meaningful, to the Christian believer today? Hugh Montefiore agrees with Paul Tillich that although the Council of Chalcedon succeeded in preserving the substance of the Christian faith, it failed to provide a conceptual framework in which we can understand the union of divine and human natures in a single person. Our task is to reinterpret Jesus Christ in the relational and functional terms that are meaningful to our age. Geoffrey Lampe would have us face squarely the subordination of God's love to justice or law implicit in much of our Atonement theology. G. F. Woods returns to remind us forcibly of the difficulty and ambiguity of Christian moral judgments, and John Burnaby deals with some of the difficulties posed for the understanding by prayer and worship in a scientific age.

The questions raised by *Soundings* are, of course, not new questions. On the whole, they have been rather neglected for several decades. Dr. Vidler, in commenting on the current theological scene in Britain, concluded, "We've got a very big leeway to make up, because there's been so much suppression of real, deep thought and intellectual alertness and integrity in the Church." [28] For the *Soundings* contributors, as for John Robinson and the journal *Prism,* the issue is whether difficult questions "remain on the fringe of the intellectual debate or are dragged into the middle and placed squarely under men's noses." [29] *Soundings* was received with respectful attention by the Church. Although its long-range effect is impossible to assess at this time, this much can be said. *Honest to God* might be dismissed by academic theologians as a popular tract. *Soundings* is a very much weightier volume. Neglected it may turn out to be, but it can scarcely be dismissed without serious consideration.

The Cambridge divinity faculty is not above trying its hand at communicating to a popular audience of sorts. During the Easter term of 1962, they sponsored a series of open lectures for the university on the general theme of moral difficulties faced by the Christian.[30] This was followed in 1963 by *Objections to Christian Belief*. In the climate produced by *Honest to God*, and to a lesser degree by *Soundings*, the published version of the lectures, again edited by Alec Vidler, attracted wide attention.

Quite independently of either Dr. Robinson or the Cambridge group, two more books appeared in 1963 which reflect some of the same concerns. *God Is No More*, by Werner and Lotte Pelz, is pessimistic about the capacity of metaphysics or theology to deal with ultimate questions of meaning. Their book is a moving and impassioned plea to take seriously the teachings of Jesus as the basis for an ethic that is radically existential and situational. In the United States, Paul Van Buren has become convinced that the language of traditional theology is no more meaningful or significant for modern secular man than the language of alchemy or astrology. "Today, we cannot even understand the Nietzschean cry that 'God is dead!' for if it were so, how could we know? No, the problem now is that the *word* 'God' is dead." [31]

If renewal and a change of direction for theology were being called for in a number of quarters, church practice has come in for searching criticism as well. Sir Richard Acland's *We Teach Them Wrong* is sharply critical of the educational work of the Church. Leslie Paul's *The Payment and Deployment of the Clergy* is the result of a careful study undertaken at the request of the Church Assembly. It analyzes in some depth, from the perspective of a lay sociologist, matters such as the deployment of clergy, the location of church buildings, and the lack of adequate training for clergy which would fit them to cope with the massive social changes taking place in twentieth-century Britain. The report calls for sweeping changes in both training and the placement of clergy that would upset many an established custom, not least patronage and the "parson's free-hold," as well as the well-nigh absolute right of tenure of an English clergyman once instituted into a living.

It has not been my intention to evaluate in any detail the diverse ideas found in this literature of protest published in the last several years. Rather, I have sought to direct attention to the ferment itself and to indicate something of its breadth and diversity. Monica Furlong, writing in *The Guardian* of January 11, 1963, observed:

The best thing about being a Christian at the moment is that organized religion has collapsed. . . . I am deeply involved in formal religion myself, owe it an overwhelming debt, and am only brash enough to scoff at it 90% of the time. But for those who have ears to hear and lips to tell it, it is common knowledge that the foundations have shivered, that there are cracks a mile wide in the walls, that the hot ashes are falling like rain upon our piety, and that the lava is curling about our sacred objects. When we try to walk in the old paths of religion we find them broken and obliterated. . . . What seems clear is that within all the denominations there is a new mutation of Christian (as yet only faintly discernible from the inert mass) who is willing and eager to question every item of his faith, who is bored to death with the old clichés, the old humbug and the great herd of sacred cows, and who believes that to disable either his mind or his senses is to dishonour Christ.[32]

"Gloriously irresponsible" such words may be, but they are splendidly adventuresome and courageous as well. They catch something of the mood of excitement and anticipation that marks the current ferment.

A New Theological Movement?

Are we seeing the birth of a new school of thought, a new theological movement, perhaps comparable to the Oxford Movement, which shocked and remade the face of the Church of England a century ago? As yet this seems most unlikely.

First of all, there is extraordinary diversity of outlook among the participants in the discussion to date. To realize this one has only to compare the essay of John Burnaby with that of H. A. Williams in *Soundings,* to read Roger Lloyd's evaluation of much of *Honest to God,* or to imagine Werner Pelz, Howard Root, and Paul Van Buren in the same room discussing what it is that is essential to Christian faith and life. The discussion, moreover, has been characterized by a striking lack of great unifying principles among the various participants. To be sure, the participants have in common dissatisfaction with the direction recent theology has taken and a healthy realism about the current religious situation in spite of surface signs of encouragement. They are also of one mind in wishing to reopen certain difficult and neglected questions. Beyond that a common mind is difficult to find. There is, moreover, no single dominant figure. Perhaps the one closest to being the intellectual leader might be Alec R. Vidler. He would be the first, however, to disclaim any such title. His role is more accurately described as that of the Socratic midwife.

The criticism by the theologians of ferment is incisive and painful, not least because it comes from within the Church and from those to whom the Church would naturally look for intellectual leadership. Is the ferment really indicative of a "failure of nerve," an unconscious atheism, as Professors Flew and MacIntyre assert? Only time can finally answer such a question. The participants themselves show a considerable degree of self-confidence and reject any such thesis. They would interpret the ferment as a sign of vitality and confidence. However others may regard them, they judge themselves as committed Christians even if they do not always find themselves able to express their faith in the traditional and conventional terms. A sense of history about theological controversy in the Church of England should make one hesitant about reading them out of the Church.[33]

The best descriptive term for the theologians of protest that we have been surveying is *Christian radical.* The word "radical" signifies one who wishes to get to the root of the matter. It has no political overtones as I am using it.[34] The term "Christian radical" enables one to take account of the many differences among the participants in the recent discussion while not forcing upon them a premature or nonexistent unity. Radicalism is a spirit, a quality of mind, rather than a precise or easily definable theological position. We are, in fact, seeing a renewed expression of the liberal spirit or liberality in Anglican theology. This is something other than the liberal theology of English Modernism, which decayed in the decades between the two great wars. English Modernism prepared the way for Christian Radicalism, but declined in influence as increasingly it came to mean a recognizable body of theological conclusions. Liberality, Dr. Vidler has pointed out, "denotes not a creed or a set of philosophical assumptions or any 'ism, but a frame of mind, a quality of character, which it is easier no doubt to discern than to define. A liberal-minded man is free from narrow prejudice, generous in his judgment of others, open-minded, especially to the reception of new ideas or proposals for reform. Liberal is the opposite not of conservative, but of fanatical or bigoted or intransigent. It points to the esprit large and away from the idée fixe." [35] Liberality, in Dr. Vidler's sense, is the most readily distinguishable feature in common among the various Christian radicals. It has an honored place in the tradition of English Christianity, and its vigorous reappearance at this time in spite of some bizzare features is a cause for rejoicing. It is of the very nature of liberality that those who exhibit this temper of mind have no interest in becoming a party or sect within the Church.

CHAPTER 8

Natural Theology: The Sick Man of Europe

THE sort of issues raised by a book like *Honest to God*—under such arresting headings as "Reluctant Revolution"; "The End of Theism?"; and, in the *Observer* article which launched the book, "Our Image of God Must Go"—reflects a widespread and growing concern on the part of many thoughtful people in the Church. Dr. Robinson has a flair for putting the matter in a vivid and provocative fashion, although he doesn't take us very far toward a solution of the difficulties. Modern man, if he bothers to think about the matter at all, feels an increasing tension between the God of traditional theism, the God "up there" or "out there," and that way of looking at the world of nature and of men which is characteristic of the scientific and secular world view. Dr. Robinson returns to the issue in his latest book, *The New Reformation?*, in an appendix entitled "Can a Truly Contemporary Person *Not* Be an Atheist?" [1] Dietrich Bonhoeffer, writing from a Nazi prison shortly before his death, had the same set of problems in mind when he pointed out that everything in the modern world, including morals and religion, seemed to get along perfectly well without "the God hypothesis." [2] Paul Van Buren implies that the problem is largely due to the fact that the traditional language found in the Bible and used in the liturgical worship of the Church and in its theology has ceased to have any meaning for modern man.[3] In the opening essay in *Soundings*, Howard Root implies that the problem is deeper than a breakdown in our understanding of religious language. "The great problem of the Church (and therefore of its theologians) is to establish or re-establish some kind of vital contact with that enormous majority of human beings for whom Christian faith is not so much unlikely as irrelevant and uninteresting," writes Dean Root. He continues: "The greatest intellectual challenge to faith is simply that thoroughly secularized intelligence which is now the rule rather than exception, whether it expresses itself in science or philosophy or politics or the arts." [4]

On the one hand, we have been surveying an era, doubtless coming to an end, in which there has been considerable theological work of real quality and significance for the life of the Church. Some are prepared to write of the renewal of the churches in the present century, and others speak boldly of a new reformation of which we are seeing the first signs. At the same time, the end of this era is clearly marked by searching questions that seem to call into question the validity of any serious theological work whatsoever. David L. Edwards has observed of the movements of thought which have been of primary concern to the Church in the last three decades: "They do not necessarily concern the truth of Christianity." [5] A biblical theology which is content to speak of the "acts of God in history" does not suffice to handle the awkward questions of whether God exists, and if so, where he is "credibly revealed in the twentieth century." Liturgical renewal will matter little in the long run unless it impels those in the fold to scatter in search of those for whom the fold itself seems a harmless and curious survival of an age long since past. The reunion of the churches as they are "could be a marriage of the senile purchased at the price of excluding the awkward questions and needs of the irreligious moderns." Consequently, Mr. Edwards urges that "a deeper renewal is needed, which may involve a costlier change." [6] The current ferment in theology points clearly to a renewed concern with philosophical or natural theology,[7] particularly as that study seeks to clarify the meaning of the language of the Bible as it finds expression in liturgical worship and in the theology of the Church. This is an area in which biblical interpretation and philosophical or natural theology converge upon the apologetic and evangelistic tasks of the Church. It is, moreover, of vital concern to every Christian who seeks to combine loyalty to the Christian faith with life in the twentieth century. Just now, the questions are a good deal clearer than any answers which may be forthcoming. If one is to appreciate the present situation and the work it seems likely to elicit, it is helpful to be aware in broad outline of some of the discussion which has taken place around such issues in the last several decades.

The Problem of Language

We have already noted that by 1939 it was clear to William Temple that the task to which he and such notable co-workers as A. E. Taylor and F. R. Tennant had devoted themselves in the field of natural theology had been overtaken by external events and by far-reaching developments in the area of philosophical studies as well.[8] Gilbert Ryle's important paper "Systematically Misleading Expressions" (1932) urged that most traditional philosophical problems could be traced to a misuse of language or naïveté. Ryle argued that paradoxes and profundities were really linguistic muddles which could be avoided by greater care in the use of language.[9] Initially, Professor Ryle's proposal seemed a modest one. The real work of philosophy was to clear up confusions in the use of language. That interest soon merged with the logical positivism of which Ryle's pupil, A. J. Ayer, became the chief spokesman. Ayer's important book *Language, Truth and Logic* (1936) pushed logical positivism as far as it would go. Ayer's contention was that statements or propositions which could not be verified empirically were simply meaningless nonsense. At one stroke, metaphysics, theology, and most of moral philosophy were ruled out of court as serious intellectual en-

terprises. "Those philosophers who fill their books with asser-
tions that they intuitively 'know' this or that moral or religious
'truth,' " wrote Ayer, "are merely providing material for the
psychoanalyst." [10] The proper task of philosophy was analysis.
Such a chilling climate was hardly conducive of fruitful discussions between philosophers and theologians.

At the very time during which logical positivism was exert-
ing its greatest influence upon British philosophy, theology
itself was becoming increasingly dubious about the importance
and validity of the whole enterprise of natural theology. Theologians were well aware that the traditional arguments for
the existence of God lacked the appeal which they had once
held for minds aware of the criticisms made against the
"proofs" in their argumentative form by Hume and Kant. The
traditional argument from prophecy to its fulfillment in Christ
and his Church was rendered suspect by the growing consensus among Old Testament scholars that the Hebrew prophets were primarily moralists pointing to God's presence and
judgment in the events of their own day, rather than seers
peering into an unknown future which they claimed to discern. New Testament scholars and theologians tended to de-
preciate the traditional appeal from miracles to the divinity of
Christ, preferring to base the claim for the Lordship of Christ
upon the evidence of the New Testament as a whole and the
continued witness of the Church to its Lord throughout its
history. Miracles, it was argued, were congruous with the portrait of Christ which emerged from the results of historical inquiry, if their possibility had been established *on other grounds.*
But those other grounds had been rendered problematical by
Hume's critique of miracles and by the apparently triumphant
success of modern science in explaining the natural world. Discussion of the problem of evil in a world created by a gracious
and loving creator was rendered increasingly difficult by the
shock of World War I, the Great Depression, and the gathering clouds of World War II. The traditional contents of a

natural theology seemed problematical all around. The older arguments no longer sufficed, and their restatement by representatives of a decaying Idealist philosophy no longer carried conviction or even great interest. The fundamental problems remained, but theology directed its attention elsewhere. The problems were not so much solved as shelved for the time being.

It was in the years just preceding and during World War II that the neo-orthodox theology exerted its greatest influence in Anglican circles.[11] If Karl Barth has never been widely read or understood in Anglican quarters, Barth's debate with his former associate Emil Brunner over the possibility and validity of any natural theology was considered of sufficient importance to warrant translation into English.[12] Barth's suspicion of any natural theology or apologetics was well known in English circles, particularly since it found clear expression in his Gifford lectures, *The Knowledge of God and the Service of God* (1938). Barth's indirect influence was to turn men's minds to the Bible and its interpretation in a biblical theology, and to render the questions of natural theology, if not suspect, at least of lesser importance and interest than the topics of dogmatic theology itself. It was also during these years that the work of Søren Kierkegaard was first made available to English readers.[13] Although Kierkegaard was well versed in the history of Western philosophical thought and made skillful use of the tools of philosophy, he was bitter in his denunciation of any accommodation of Christian faith to a philosophical system which sought to absorb and "understand" it.[14] Kierkegaard was convinced that this inevitably meant dissolving the paradoxical character of Christianity as a faith that required the leap which took one beyond the bounds of rational inquiry. The effect of such developments in the theological realm was not so much to convince theologians that natural theology was invalid as to render the pursuit of its questions relatively less interesting and urgent than they had been regarded by previous generations. The attention of the better minds was directed elsewhere for the most part, and natural theology fell into neglect.

Not everyone followed the prevailing trend. Austin Farrer's *Finite and Infinite* appeared in 1943 and anticipates in an interesting manner some of the postwar discussion. It is an involved and difficult book, which, perhaps for this reason, has not received wide attention. The same year saw the publication of E. L. Mascall's *He Who Is,* which, with his earlier *Existence and Analogy,*[15] represents an attempt to reformulate much of the content of natural theology, specifically the traditional "proofs" and the analogy of being, in a way which took account of some of the problems being posed in philosophical circles. It is fair to say, however, that both Farrer and Mascall at that time, together with Dorothy Emmett in her *Nature of Metaphysical Thinking* (1949), had not taken full account of the philosophical objections to any work in metaphysics or philosophical theology. Each author still felt able to move with confidence within the framework of traditional theism.

Turning to books with an avowed apologetic intention, we note the several books of J. V. Langmead Casserley, notably *The Christian in Philosophy* (1951), *The Retreat from Christianity* (1952), and, most recently, *Apologetics and Evangelism* (1962). Professor Casserley knows his way along the highways and byways of Western thought, and has a keen appreciation of the contributions which classical Christianity has made to its development. He is also very much aware of the intellectual challenges to that faith, particularly in the eighteenth and nineteenth centuries. He has declined to enter into a discussion of the present meaning of theological statements and prefers to illustrate historically their significance and relevance in the development of Western thought. In the end, Professor Casserley is content to rest his case on the strength of a perennial philosophy, strongly Platonist and Augustinian in flavor, and on classical Christian orthodoxy to withstand the present and, he believes, transient challenge of the analytic philosophers.

Alan Richardson's *Christian Apologetics* (1947) is fascinating for the light it throws on the postwar malaise in apologetics. First, he asks us to consider theology a historical science, fully as rigorous and empirical in method as any other scholarly discipline and as its particular subject matter allows. He then seeks to clarify what is for him the fundamental theological category, revelation, and to discuss the nature of that revelation given in history which the Bible records. Much depends upon Dean Richardson's view of the nature of history as involving events and their interpretation in an indissoluble unity, a theme to which he returns in his *History, Sacred and Profane* (1962). For Dean Richardson, a statement such as "God is love" is not primarily a theological assertion or a proposition open to clarification by linguistic analysis, but rather a historical statement to be elucidated by the biblical data. If philosophers and others wish to understand it, they must first do their historical homework with the Old and New Testament scholars.[16] The book has a suggestive discussion of the way in which the traditional arguments from miracle and from prophecy might be reformulated in the light of contemporary critical biblical scholarship, and concludes with a perceptive analysis of the relation of faith and reason as formulated by St. Augustine. It is not without significance that this was the last book clearly falling in the area of apologetics which Dean Richardson has chosen to write. Having cleared the ground, as it were, and warned analytic philosophers that their awkward questions about the reality of God and the meaning of theological statement are off limits, he has devoted himself to the work of biblical theology, where he has made significant contributions.[17]

By the time that dialogue between philosophers and theologians was resumed in a meaningful way in the 1950's, the climate in philosophy had changed markedly. Those interested in metaphysics, morals, and theology had refused to heed the strictures of the strict logical positivists that they were talking or writing nonsense, even if, from time to time, it might prove to be important or useful nonsense. Affected in large measure by the later work of Ludwig Wittgenstein, philosophers came to seek not the elimination, but the elucidation, of metaphysical and theological language.[18] Symptomatic of the shift in mood was John Wisdom's paper "Gods," first published in 1945. Increasingly, philosophers were inclined to ask: What kind of meaning is, or can be claimed for, theological statement? What sort of evidence, and in what circumstances, would count decisively for or against a theological statement? Does the Christian's faith (and the atheist's or agnostic's lack of faith) have any connection with events taking place in the natural world? If so, what kind(s) of connection? Such questions clearly begin in the area of natural theology and quickly open into a discussion of most of the topics of dogmatic theology and of philosophy as well. The discussion since *New Essays in Philosophical Theology* (1955) has been much too varied and sometimes too technical to lend itself to brief summary.[19] Two points of the utmost importance emerge from the discussions. One is that the age-old and important dialogue between philosophy and theology has once again been resumed, albeit with indecisive results—a fact which will scarcely surprise one familiar with that dialogue in the past. The second is that theology is being challenged as it has not been for centuries to clarify the meaning of the language which it habitually uses and takes for granted. Nothing but good should result from both such developments.

Discussions between philosophers and theologians over the meaning and niceties of theological language may seem far removed from the day-to-day activities of the Church and the business of striving to live the Christian life as best one can.

Hugh Montefiore implies that the impass which currently afflicts many thoughtful Christians is primarily an intellectual one which need not affect Christian worship or the day-to-day business of living.[20] Others are by no means so sure, however. Howard Root insists that Christian theology without natural theology is an illusion. "If the only grounds for belief in the Christian revelation are part of that alleged revelation," he writes, "the theologian has cut himself off from profitable communication with people who wish to think about their beliefs." [21] Then, the choice of Christianity, or some other religion, or of none at all becomes "arbitrary, irrational, even trivial." In a somewhat different context, Ninian Smart observes:

It must be remembered that rarely do religious reasonings persuade individuals to change their faith. But this does not mean that they are useless. For without reasons and evidences there cannot be such a thing as truth; and without truth there can be no belief. Moreover, we find that, as in aesthetics and in philosophy, reasonings have a long-term effect. What occurs is a kind of social dialogue. In the course of time certain views seem to gather persuasiveness while others fade into implausibility. Reasonings are by no means irrelevant to this process.[22]

The decay of natural theology has had much to do with the widespread assumption that Christianity is largely a matter of personal preference rather than a courageous witness to the truth which determines for the believer his system of values, the way in which he views the world, and the way in which he seeks to treat other persons. Gradually, at times almost imperceptively, Christian faith has been "fading into implausibility" for countless people in a secular, scientifically oriented age. Worship and Christian morals will not long survive in the life of a person in whom such a shift has or is taking place. Natural theology, then, is of vital importance both for the Church and for many an individual Christian. It is generally assumed that its primary thrust is toward the "outsider," its objective being to persuade him of the cogency of the Christian position as opposed to the one he presently occupies. I am inclined to agree with Professor Smart that "rarely do religious reasonings persuade individuals to change their faith." It is closer to the truth to regard the enterprise of natural theology as an already existing faith seeking to understand itself in rational terms. It is the natural business of those Christians who seek to love God with their minds. The religious form of the cosmological, teleological, and moral arguments occurs repeatedly in the Psalms, the concluding chapters of the book of Job, and in numerous oracles of the Hebrew prophets.[23] It is worth reflection that Anselm's closely reasoned formulation of the ontological argument is set in the context of a prayer offered to God.[24] It is because the believer senses that the so-called "proofs" are not really proofs at all but exercises of faith seeking to understand itself in intellectual terms that he is unshaken by the logical criticism of the "proofs" and by their failure to convince the skeptic immediately. This view of the traditional "proofs" and of religious reasonings in general helps to account for the fact that such reasonings persist when, by all the rules of logical discourse, they should have been dead and buried long ago. Also accounted for is the fact that men continue to feel that such reasonings are a matter of great importance about which they feel passionately. It does not deliver the natural theologian from the difficult task of aiming at the utmost clarity and rigor in his reasonings nor spare him the astringent criticisms of his philosophically minded colleagues. It does free him from the necessity of success, if success be taken to mean the conversion of the skeptic to the Christian faith. If that takes place, reasonings will play their part, but only a part, in the process.

Attempts at Solution

It would be misleading to suggest that concern for the clarification of the meaning of religious language has been exclusively the preoccupation of philosophical theologians. The question has been raised forcefully by those engaged in biblical interpretation as well. Professor Ryle's conclusion that "we can ask what is the real form of the fact recorded when this is concealed or disguised and not duly exhibited by the expression in question . . . and we can often succeed in stating this fact in a new form of words which does exhibit what the other failed to exhibit" could well be taken as a description of Rudolf Bultmann's striking proposal of the necessity to "demythologize" the essential message, or kerygma, contained in the New Testament.[25] Bultmann's famous essay "The New Testament and Mythology" was published in Germany during World War II and immediately touched off a heated controversy which has continued down to the present.[26] It was not until the early 1950's that Bultmann's essay became available in English and began to affect discussions in the English-speaking world to a marked extent.

Professor Bultmann is convinced that the obviously mythical setting in which the New Testament message is delivered and preserved poses a well-nigh insuperable stumbling block to the intelligence of modern man. At the same time, the mythology is not essential to the message. The older liberalism erred in that in seeking to remove the mythology, the miraculous, and the eschatological setting in which the gospel message was delivered, it seriously distorted the gospel message as well. If it is to make its appeal to modern man, the gospel must be translated into categories which he can understand and respond to. Bultmann believes that such a translation can be effected without distorting the gospel message itself, and that the categories of the existentialist philosophy of Martin Heidegger provide precisely the categories needed. When the New Testament message is so "translated," it "frees men for the future" and makes possible an "authentic existence" before God. A brief summary cannot do justice to the subtleties of Bultmann's position nor to the numerous objections which his proposal has evoked.

English readers have cause to be grateful to Bultmann for raising anew the question of the mythological setting in which the gospel is found in the New Testament, the difficulties which the theological liberals fell into in seeking to remove the mythical elements, and his vigorous insistence upon the existential or personal significance of the New Testament message. They have questioned whether it is necessary or possible to remove all of the mythology and whether, in fact, Bultmann succeeds in doing so. They also question whether one must become an existentialist, as Bultmann implies, in order to be a Christian, or, if you prefer, the adequacy of an existentialist philosophy as the only vehicle of the Christian message for modern man.[27]

If Bultmann offers essentially a gospel without myth translated into the categories of an existentialist philosophy, Paul Van Buren in his *Secular Meaning of the Gospel* attempts a similar exercise in translation in a different direction. Dr. Van Buren has been deeply influenced by the work of analytic philosophy in the last several decades. His stance is that of a thorough-going secularist for whom the language of "other worldliness" and "transcendence" has no empirical basis in experience and thus no possibility of verification or meaning. Only those theological statements which have an empirical basis are allowable. Christian faith must be translated into categories which are exclusively contemporary and this-worldly, or secular, in their significance. No other language has any real meaning, and the sooner theology wakes up to this fact, the better it can do its real task. To be sure, this drastically reduces the content of meaningful theological discourse, but such a reduction is what every science has experienced when it became truly scientific, that is, radically empirical in its methodology. We must be grateful to Dr. Van Buren for putting the objections of analytic philosophy and of secularism to traditional religious language with unusual clarity and force. We can also be grateful for his vigorous insistence on taking with the utmost seriousness the contemporary and this-worldly, or secular, significance of the Christian message. By pushing his line of inquiry to its logical conclusion, he has rendered a real service in demonstrating the limitations of his proposal by the very paucity of his results.[28] What remains has ceased to be recognizably Christian or gospel. The aridity of Van Buren's secularism is such that existentialism and much contemporary humanism are concerned to protest against it.[29] As the necessary precondition for the Christian faith in the modern world, it is singularly unappealing and unconvincing. Others share Van Buren's concern to take this world with utter seriousness, but they do not feel the necessity to be condemned to his essentially agnostic conclusions about the possibility of either faith or theology.[30]

Although written in English over the last several decades, Paul Tillich's major work has not been widely read or discussed in British theological circles until relatively recently.[31] In spite of the numerous references in *Honest to God,* and possibly because of them, the initial response in England has been largely negative.[32] Readers of *Honest to God* have become familiar with Professor Tillich's insistence that God is not a being, but the one whose originating and sustaining creativity makes possible whatever has being. God is not a person, but rather the ground and source of the personal. They will also recall the proposal that metaphors of depth be utilized to convey a sense of the transcendence of God where the more traditional metaphors of height no longer have the meaning they once had. It is significant that in those portions of his argument where he is most indebted to Professor Tillich, Dr.

Robinson felt it necessary to guard himself against the charge of pantheism, and that more than one critic questioned whether Dr. Robinson had succeeded in preserving the character of God as personal, in spite of repeated verbal protestations that he wished to. It seems to be the case that one may read both Professor Tillich and Dr. Robinson and reach either a theist or a nontheist conclusion—clear evidence that the positions of both require further clarification. One must question whether Dr. Robinson's judgment concerning the success with which the language of transcendence has been preserved and expressed for modern man by Tillich can survive close analysis.[33]

Be that as it may, Paul Tillich has written extensively on the matter of religious language, and it behooves British theologians to read him before dismissing him as a "nineteenth-century thinker" or another of those obscure German theologians who delight in obscurities because they have not been led to clarity of language by heeding the work of the linguistic analysts. Instead of Bultmann's proposal, Tillich would have us frankly recognize the mythical character of the New Testament and to "deliteralize" it, that is, take its mythology and its symbolism not literally but seriously, to pay close attention to what it is that the mythology seeks to convey.[34] To demythologize is to imply that one can get along without the distinctive language of religion, but it is precisely this assumption that Tillich questions. Translation into another realm of discourse involves the loss of the power of religious language to evoke a sense of the presence of that which it seeks to convey. More often than not, when one thinks he has demythologized a passage, he has simply substituted one mythology for another, the mythology of depth psychology or of Heidegger's existentialism, for example. A most illuminating discussion of religious symbols is found in *Dynamics of Faith* (1957).[35] The distinction between signs and symbols is made, and the property of symbols to disclose dimensions of experience not otherwise accessible to man is discussed, as well as the birth and death of symbols and the impossibility of consciously constructing fresh ones. Professor Tillich's insistence that a genuine symbol participates in that which it symbolizes cries out for clarification. Nevertheless, the discussion is illuminating, and the basic point that symbols must be "broken," that is, seen as symbols which one sees through rather than criticizes on the literal level, is a salutary reminder of the "odd" character of religious language in general. Professor Tillich's attempt to understand the meaning and function of religious language in its historical setting and to correlate such meanings with the often-hidden questions posed by modern man provides an alternative to the apparent iconoclasm of Bultmann or Van Buren.[36]

Professor Ian Ramsey's *Religious Language* (1957) has proved to be a major contribution to the clarification of the nature and function of the language of religion. The subtitle of the book, "An Empirical Placing of Theological Phrases," leads one to expect an illustration of linguistic analysis at work. The results are illuminating and suggestive. Professor Ramsey contends that it is the nature of religious language to use words and phrases from everyday speech, but in such a manner that one cannot take the language at face value. The "odd" character of such language alerts one to the fact that the one using it is seeking to convey more than a literal understanding of the words and phrases would convey. The purpose of such language is to evoke or elicit situations of disclosure and discernment in which one sees what one has been unaware of previously. Such situations of discernment would seem to be closely akin to moments of "insight" which occur in the process of psychotherapy. Frequently, nothing new is added to the material under consideration. It is in the rearrangement or juxtaposition of familiar pieces of the puzzle that "the ice melts," and one suddenly says, "Of course, now I see, how obvious!" or something similar. A situation of disclosure carries with it a moral imperative or commitment. In the religious situation of discernment, one finds oneself saying not only, "Now I see" but also, "This I must do." The application of this way of regarding religious language illuminates many a theological phrase as well as numerous passages in the Bible, as Professor Ramsey demonstrates.[37] The analysis needs to be pushed further, however, if one is to form any clear notion of who or what is disclosed other than moral obligation. In a word, the analysis is more illuminating for morality than for theology. Nevertheless, in the present period of uncertainty and perplexity, we are grateful for whatever light there is to be shed.

We have from time to time been critical of the relative isolation of biblical theology and of its apparent willingness to ignore the vexing questions posed by natural theology. It is fair to say that the work of the theologians we have been surveying has been carried on largely in ignorance of the labors of the biblical scholars, with the exception of Bultmann, of course. There is weight to Alan Richardson's insistence that many a theological assertion is at bottom a historical statement, and that an urgent question which must be reopened is the nature and extent to which Christianity is a historical religion. This, in turn, raises the question of the nature of history itself, and the extent to which the Bible is the record of historical events— questions which bristle with ambiguities and confusions.[38] Professors Bultmann, Van Buren, Tillich, and Ramsey have not come to grips with the historical question at the depth required. Until this is done, any work on the meaning of religious language must remain at best fragmentary and inconclusive.

The Challenge to Imagination

It would indeed be pleasant if, after such a survey, one could conclude with a series of constructive suggestions. At the present juncture, this writer finds himself unable to do so. One might record Austin Farrer's distinctions about the dimensions of modern man's difficulties with the language of religion, distinctions which are at once subtle and practical in their implications.[39] One who has no desire to be classified as a neo-orthodox theologian must still observe that that theology demonstrated powerfully both the theological and practical limitations of the earlier liberal theology, particularly in accommodating itself so completely to the modern mind that it lost its capacity constructively to criticize certain assumptions of modern man at a time when such criticism was urgently needed.[40] It is somewhat surprising to find Dr. Robinson and Dr. Van Buren apparently turning down pathways which have so recently proved to be blind alleys.

Religious language, whether it be the language of the Bible and of liturgical worship or the more prosaic and, hopefully, precise language of theology, attempts the impossible, and yet necessary, task of speaking of God and his ways in the words of men, by means of analogies and symbols drawn from human experience. To express what is ultimately inexpressible places an extraordinary burden on language. Small wonder, then, that as T. S. Eliot puts it:

> . . . words strain,
> Crack and sometimes break under the burden,
> Under the tension, slip, slide, perish,
> Decay with imprecision, will not stay in place.[41]

The language of religion must be highly metaphorical, analogical, narrative, dramatic, and symbolic. At its authentic best, it is, as Rudolf Otto described it, "numinous poetry." Analyze it we must, but at the same time realizing that it does not lend itself to translation into some other realm of discourse without losing something of its distinctive character. It need not be taken literally, but it demands to be taken seriously if it is to be understood. We may expect such language to prove difficult for a prosaic age whose taste is largely shaped by the purveyors of mass culture. What is required all around is genuine openness to the various necessary attempts at translation, together with a wariness about incautious and complete capitulations to the dominant assumptions of this or any other era of human thought.

To a considerable extent, the malaise which afflicts many a Christian intellectual is a failure of the imagination on the part of minds numbed by the assumptions of an apparently omnicompetent science and technology. This state of mind has been accentuated by the extent to which academic theology has cut itself off from creative dialogue with the various sciences, contemporary literature, and the arts.[42] It is precisely here that lay theologians may yet supply what an academic theology has neglected to its impoverishment. It is part of the achievement of Charles Williams to have presented in his novels Christian virtue in a singularly effective manner, personified in authentic and appealing characters. The poetry of T. S. Eliot sometimes succeeds in making Christian faith imaginable for modern man to an extent unmatched by most theologians and would-be apologists. Urgently needed are those whose professional competence includes not only theology but other fields of human inquiry as well, particularly in the sciences.[43] Natural theology has need to broaden its field of interest and to resume dialogue with the sciences and the arts as well as with philosophy. Such dialogue cannot and should not be confined to those who are avowedly Christian in their commitment.

One rejoices that natural theology has again resumed its difficult yet essential work, but at the same time, one regrets that
the results to date are hauntingly fragmentary and inconclusive.
Constructive work in this field is of primary importance. One
may hope that those most dissatisfied with the results of recent
years will place us in their debt by hastening to supply what
has so far been lacking.

CHAPTER 9

Morality in a Post-Christian Society

IT IS fashionable nowadays to bemoan the state of Christian ethics and moral theology.[1] The legacy of social concern so ably championed in generations past by F. D. Maurice, Charles Gore, and William Temple has no present-day spokesman of their undisputed stature. The Christendom group, of which M. B. Reckitt and V. A. Demant have been outstanding spokesmen, has dispersed and is no longer widely influential.[2] Kenneth Kirk made a gallant effort to revive a distinctively Anglican tradition of moral theology in the 1920's and early 1930's. His successors have proven rather more magisterial and inflexible than their distinguished mentor, and the very possibility or validity of moral theology now requires an apologia or defense.[3] The paper on Christian ethics is no longer a requirement for the General Ordination Examinations in the Church of England, and at least one university lecturer in divinity recently wrote that "probably 95 per cent of present-day ordinands are incapable of intelligently advising on or teaching Christian ethics or of defending them, except by repeating dogmatically and inaccurately the little they remember of what they have picked up in the same fashion."[4] The day is past when appeals to the authority of the Church or even "the teaching of our Lord" would suffice as the basis of Christian moral principles. The present generation demands answers to the questions: "Why shouldn't I?" and "What is wrong with it?" and is impatient with unreasonable or merely authoritarian replies. "There is no need to prove that a revolution is required in morals," writes J. A. T. Robinson.

158

"It has long since broken out: and it is no 'reluctant revolution.' The wind of change here is a gale." [5] It is widely assumed in church circles that "the new morality" [6] is merely a convenient rationalization for a grievous relaxing of the traditional restraints, particularly as regards sexual behavior. "The new morality" is taken to mean an invitation to laxity, and, it is assumed, "the apostles of love" are leading in the rout of Christian standards.[7] Although the present writer agrees that there are no grounds for complacency, the word "crisis" means opportunity as well as danger. The present situation does not require an exclusively pessimistic interpretation, and scarcely justifies the sometimes fanatical opposition that the so-called "new morality" has evoked in certain quarters. Our predicament is rather more complex than such criticism often implies.

Concern for Moral Issues

Men of the stature of Maurice, Gore, and Temple are rare in the history of the Church in any country, and it is scarcely to be expected that each succeeding generation will produce men of comparable stature. Moreover, their legacy of social thought and witness was not without its shortcomings. When Maurice sought to translate his principles into action, he encountered widespread misunderstanding and opposition. His most sympathetic interpreters would agree that it was in the realm of social theory, together with its theological basis, rather than in practice, that his major contributions lay. Gore's influence was chiefly due to the extraordinary force of his personality. His was truly "the soul of a prophet." His writing on social issues was largely occasional and unsystematic and is no longer widely read or influential. Although it is undoubtedly true that the emergence of the modern British welfare state owes much to the legacy of social concern as it came to be summed up and exemplified in the person of William Temple, Temple's social thought was not without its difficulties and perplexities.[8] The notion that one may find, in the past one hundred years, a consistent and coherent body of Christian social principles which may with readiness be applied to contemporary problems is one which does not survive careful examination. A suggestive methodology, fruitful analyses and insights, a passion for the cause of justice among the poor and dispossessed, the burning conviction that the Christian message demands social expression, and a remarkable freedom from the dominant assumptions of a bourgeois society intent on maintaining the privileges of the status quo—such is the legacy from these giants of the past.

We have reason to be grateful for the social concern which found expression in the writings of the Christendom group. At the same time, it is increasingly clear that its progressive loss of influence, and the apparent drying up of the tradition itself among a younger generation, indicate serious shortcomings which prevented a more realistic and effective social witness. It is altogether salutary to remind us, as D. L. Munby has recently done, that there is no substitute for the patient study of empirical data. The very word "Christendom" implies a deference for theology which the autonomous social sciences no longer can or should be expected to offer. It is unlikely that the social sciences will pay much attention to a "Christian Sociology" until its advocates relinquish their assumption that theological correctness is a sufficient substitute for technical competence and empirical knowledge.[9]

The postwar era is one in which an effective social witness on the part of the institutional church has proved to be increasingly difficult. The emergence of the omnicompetent welfare state has rendered many an old battleground obsolete. In Britain and America, the Church has to a considerable extent remained the captive of a middle- and upper-class society in an economy of increasing affluence. Overseas, the Church has all too often been associated in the popular mind with colonialism and economic exploitation. In spite of the coura-

geous witness of individuals, the Church has not so far succeeded in effectively engaging the power structures of a technological society in creative dialogue, nor has it been in the
forefront of significant social change. It has cared but not cared
deeply enough, nor has it been sufficiently venturesome and
imaginative in devising forms to make its concern effective in
the modern world.

At the same time, there has been a good deal of constructive thinking going on that is devoted to the task of assisting
Christians to assume more effectively their responsibilities as
members of the social order. As the Oxford Conference on
Life and Work (1937) and William Temple had clearly perceived, Christians must work out "middle axioms," that is,
working principles which are of practical use to them in their
efforts to transform society in a direction at once more humane
and Christian.[10] Such middle axioms require respect for empirical data and a realism about the methods by which change
is accomplished in the political arena. They cannot be formulated by churchmen sitting in council, nor can they be laid
down by clergy for the laity. If they are to be developed at all,
such work must be carried on by those who possess the necessary competence and experience. Examples of the kind of
thinking which has been taking place, thinking which reflects
political realism informed by Christian insights, may be
found in the *Christian News-Letter,* now combined with the
journal *Frontier,* in Britain and *Christianity and Crisis* in the
United States.

Expanding knowledge and techniques, particularly in the
field of medicine, have enlarged the area of human freedom
and, consequently, the field of responsible moral decision.
Social change and revolutionary developments in the sciences,
for example, in nuclear physics, have necessitated the consideration of moral problems which could not have arisen in
their present form in an earlier age. Some of the discussion
has been carried on by individuals with no little success.[11]

Even more constructive has been the work of task forces, called into being for the discussion of specific problems, and numbering among the members both Christians and non-Christians, the *sine qua non* for participation being moral seriousness and professional competence in one or more aspects of the problem under discussion. Such groups in England have produced reports, usually published in pamphlet form, on such subjects as *Sexual Offenders and Social Punishment* (1956) and *What Is Lawful?* (1959), both dealing with the ethical problems raised by homosexuality; together with *Ought Suicide to be a Crime?* (1959); *Artificial Insemination by Donor* (1960); *Personal Responsibilities: Two Bibliographies* (1960); *Sterilization: An Ethical Inquiry* (1962); *Punishment* (1963); and *Decisions Concerning Life and Death* (1965).[12] Aside from the merits of the particular reports, and they are generally of high quality, the significant point to be noted is that a new method of ethical inquiry is being developed equal to the explosion of human knowledge and the complexities of modern life. This is a fact of the utmost importance.

A somewhat similar development may be traced so far as the moral tensions and perplexities experienced by the individual Christian in his particular vocation or work is concerned. One who takes seriously the claim of moral obligations soon discovers that modern life produces innumerable conflicts between the various loyalties and obligations that one experiences as a responsible person in society. Furthermore, one must examine not only the often-conflicting claims of moral obligations but also the facts of the situation in which he is called to act responsibly. These are likely to be increasingly complicated in the modern world. If Z means any Christian man or woman with his or her network of claims, loyalties, and responsibilities, we must inquire "What does Z do?"; and this generally means "How does Z find out what he ought to do?" [13] The Church cannot provide Z with a comprehensive manual or code of Christian conduct which will tell him in advance what ought to be done in each specific situation. Z must make his own decisions responsibly, under God, and in the midst of the specific situation. Still, there is a good deal of general guidance which can be offered to Z, and Alec Vidler, for one, is prepared to spell this out in some detail.[14] Furthermore, Dr. Vidler offers for Z's consideration an account of the Christian Frontier Council and its method of developing "frontier groups," a method adaptable to any group of persons seeking concrete guidance as to their social and political responsibilities. Briefly, the proposal is that Christians sharing particular problems or responsibilities should come together on a regular basis for the mutual exploration of their situation in all its complexity and to discover clarification and insight for the tasks at hand through mutual discussion, encouragement, and study. Dr. Vidler believes that "divine enlightenment is more likely to come to all of us if we are fertilizing one another's minds and checking one another's judgment than if we are each left to depend on our own individual powers of intellect or intuition."[15] This is not simply a good idea which might be worth trying out some day, but one which has been widely developed and used in the last several decades in the lay academies in Europe, the various industrial missions in Britain and the United States, and at various ecumenical-conference centers. It is a form which does not need to wait upon the approval and leadership of the institutional church, nor does it require any particular facilities. It is a method usually flexible and adaptable. It is important to note that such a development is rooted in the context in which day-by-day moral decisions must be made, and that it is primarily lay centered and lay oriented.

The Church's witness to society is never a simple task; and in every age, new problems have a way of outrunning the resources available from the past. The modern world poses peculiar difficulties for the Church and for the individual

Christian wishing to exercise social and political responsibility. If certain of the sources to which an earlier generation turned for authoritative guidance no longer prove as helpful as they once did, there are encouraging signs that new methods and forms are being developed in the Church's life. Particularly encouraging is the emphasis being placed upon professional competence and respect for empirical data in forming moral judgments, and the realistic and practical character of much of the work being done, due in no small measure to the active involvement of laymen in the discussions.

The Decline of Moral Theology

Turning to the discipline of moral theology per se, it is worth noting that its decline in influence is a fact widely lamented but much less widely understood. Part of the difficulty is that the discipline tends to become too narrow, clerical, and academic. Much of the material considered in the reports issued by the various task forces commented on above, together with the kinds of problems of conscience frequently discussed by "frontier groups," might be considered the province of the moral theologian. The difficulty has been that the moral theologian more often than not has not been present where the problems have arisen and are under discussion. Moreover, the discipline has not succeeded in keeping sufficiently abreast of empirical data and the complexities of contemporary life to offer the kind of specific guidance which is required. It is worth observing that seventeenth-century moralists such as Sanderson, Hall, Baxter, and Jeremy Taylor were first of all experienced pastors, and thus in close contact with the lives of those whom they presumed to guide with moral counsel. Involvement in concrete situations is important if moral guidance is to be of practical use to the perplexed.

Another facet of the current discontent with the state of moral theology is no doubt due to the fact that Kenneth E. Kirk (1886-1954) performed his chosen task so well. His successors have, in a measure, suffered by comparison with their mentor. Although not without his rigidities, Kirk was able to combine an astonishingly learned and skillful application of the materials of the Christian heritage, both biblical and historical, with a genuine openness to knowledge derived from contemporary work in psychology and, to a lesser degree, sociology. This gave to his consideration of moral problems a depth and relevance rarely matched by his successors. This method of combining the best insights of the Christian tradition with the empirical data made available by the social sciences must be the method of any moral theology of consequence. Psychology and sociology have made impressive strides in the half-century since Kirk began his work, and there is urgent need that his method be utilized in doing for the present generation the task he so ably performed for his own.[16] Such a method disarms much of the criticism of traditional moral theology, namely, that "there is too much law in it, too many hair-splitting legal distinctions, too much deduction from fixed principles, too little attention to empirical evidence (for instance, in psychology and sociology), too simple a notion of the term 'natural,' and too little concern for perfection as against minimum obligations." [17] Really to take full account of empirical evidence introduces an element of flexibility which, in the long run, would involve a reformulation of the very basis of the discipline. It is doubtful if Kirk realized the full implications of his method, any more than Charles Gore perceived the revolutionary implications of his acceptance of the historical-critical method. It is certain that successors of Kirk such as R. C. Mortimer and Lindsay Dewar have devoted relatively more effort to being faithful to the traditions of the past then they have to careful attention to the empirical data made available by recent studies in psychology and sociology. Indeed, one notes in their work a certain impatience with empirical data and a certain skepticism about its importance for their research.[18] As a consequence, much recent work in moral theology has seemed merely traditional and unimportant to an age which insists on respect for the facts of human experience and instinctively senses that persons matter more than the principles laid down by a former age. In discussing the old rule concerning means and ends, Kirk wrote: "The correct form of the maxim, in fact, is 'circumstances alter cases.' . . . An act which is right in some circumstances may be wrong in others." In commenting on the point, Joseph Fletcher has observed: "However, be it noted, he did not say that an act which is *wrong* in some cases can be right in others. His bid for freedom was too faint-hearted." [19] Be that as it may, moral theology must pay closer attention to empirical data and to those circumstances surrounding moral problems which alter cases if it hopes to have a hearing in the discussion of the moral perplexities of the modern world.

At still another point, the legacy of Kenneth Kirk is instructive, namely, his suggestion that an important difference between Roman Catholic and Anglican approaches to the subject lay in the fact that Roman Catholic moral theology arose out of the requirements of the confessional, and thus devoted primary attention to what was lawful or permissible. Anglican moralists such as Sanderson, Hall, and Jeremy Taylor were primarily concerned with the nurture of the Christian life, and, consequently, devoted their chief attention to the Christian virtues and the means by which they might be elicited and encouraged.[20] The two approaches are not mutually exclusive to be sure. Nevertheless, there is a marked difference in the mood and direction of the two types of moral theology when they are compared. It is the difficult task of the moral theologian, and of the pastor and preacher, not only to rebuke evil where it is encountered and to offer guidance for perplexed consciences but also to present that style of life which befits a Christian, and the distinctive virtues which accompany it, in such a way that they inspire men's imagination and zeal to realize such a style in their own lives. This further involves the task of encouraging those habits and dispositions which will make such a realization possible. It is very much easier to preach against the evils of human nature than to present real goodness in such attractive terms that men and women feel drawn to it and inspired to make the necessary sacrifices to bring its realization to pass in their own lives. In this connection, a slim volume, *Traditional Virtues Reassessed* (1964),[21] is worthy of comment. The virtues reassessed are scarcely those which have an immediate appeal to a secular-minded age, including as they do, innocence, gentleness, chastity, modesty, temperance, piety, obedience, prudence, patriotism, justice, and felicity. There is the unevenness that one expects in a composite volume. What is striking is the theological acumen, psychological insight, and realism of most of the essays. These are not virtues for a bygone age or for the cloister. They are the virtues to be desired by sensitive, perceptive men and women who are fully conscious of what life in the twentieth century involves. Here are examples of "holy worldliness" in the best sense.

The most recent book of consequence in moral theology is Herbert Waddams's *A New Introduction to Moral Theology* (1964). It is a real contribution, taking account of and avoiding many of the criticisms of the discipline which have been made in the recent past. At the same time, Canon Waddams has given us a companion volume, *Life and Fire of Love* (1964),[22] an examination of prayer and its presuppositions— clear indication that in his mind the traditional disciplines of moral and ascetical theology must be taken as parts of a single whole. It is fair to say that Canon Waddams's books will find a ready audience among clergy and among that portion of the laity which is consciously a part of the "gathered church" and has the leisure to read books of this sort. He succeeds as well as anyone probably can in interpreting the method and terms of traditional moral and ascetical theology for churchmen in the modern world. It implies no lack of appreciation of Canon

Waddams's accomplishment to urge that more than this is needed to meet the requirements of the Church as *diaspora,* that is, "scattered," and exercising its mission in a largely indifferent world. *Honest to God* provides some suggestive hints of the outlines of a life of prayer on the part of one immersed in the concerns of this world.[23] One hopes that others will follow up the lines of thought there suggested, recognizing that what is required is a way of life, and the means for achieving it, which is a complement rather than an alternative to the more traditional patterns developed over the centuries for the "gathered church." A *worldly divinity* in the sense of a divinity adequate to meet the needs of Christians actively engaged in the concerns and affairs of this world, *and who see such activity as the natural expression of their Christian vocation,* is what is required. It is in this light that one is to understand Joseph Fletcher's call for moral theology which is "case-focussed and concrete, concerned to bring Christian imperatives into practical operation." Such a "neo-casuistry repudiates the attempt to anticipate or prescribe real-life decisions in their existential particularity." [24] Thus, "Christian ethics is not a scheme of codified conduct. It is a purposive effort to relate love to a world of relativities through a casuistry of love. Moral theology seeks to work out love's strategy and casuistry devises its tactics." [25] We are, in fact, seeing a good deal of work being done in the area of moral theology by those who are not accustomed to speak of themselves as moral theologians. What is emerging is a moral theology which is concerned to be thoroughly empirical, professionally competent, lay oriented, and which takes the situation in which moral decisions must be made with the utmost seriousness. Moreover, the new moralists follow St. Paul in affirming that "He who loves his neighbor has satisfied every claim of the law" (Rom. 14:8).

The Continuing Problem

When Dietrich Bonhoeffer wrote from prison that man has "come of age," he had in mind the fact that modern man, thanks to the developments in modern science and technology, possesses a degree of mastery over his natural environment undreamed of in an earlier age. The almost incredible power which modern man now possesses coincides with an era in which man has largely freed himself from subjection to moralisms, that is, moral and legal codes, imposed by authority, which are felt to be alien to man's true nature.[26] Bonhoeffer's plea is that man acknowledge the call to a life of responsible freedom possible in the modern world. The moralisms of an earlier age, whatever their sources and sanctions, have lost their grip upon modern man. They no longer enkindle his zeal or command his loyalty. Increasingly, they are experienced as an alien law, strange to man's true nature. It is of the utmost importance that Christians do not confuse the moralisms of the past with authentic Christian morality, and thus allow themselves to be trapped into a blind and fanatical opposition to the changes which are taking place all about them. It is probably inevitable that more-conservative portions of the Church regard the efforts of certain moralists to come to grips with, and to interpret, the changes which are taking place as outright apostasy. That is clearly not their intent, however, nor has convincing evidence been forthcoming to show that this is the direction in which their thought points. Dr. Robinson, for one, is convinced that the "old morality" and the "new morality" represent "two starting points, two approaches to certain perennial polarities in Christian ethics, which are not antithetical but complementary. Each begins from one point without denying the other, but each tends to suspect the other of abandoning what it holds most vital because it reaches it from the other end." [27] Perhaps. But there was a life-and-death struggle between Jesus and the Pharisees and between St. Paul and the Judaizers. In any event, Dr. Robinson pleads for patience and mutual understanding on both sides, since the representatives of old and new, conservatives and liberals, need the other's complementary insights and emphases as correctives.

The booklet *Christian Morals Today* (1964) is a beautifully clear and irenic statement of three of the tensions or polarities which have been particularly evident in discussions since the appearance of *Soundings* and *Honest to God*. The polarities outlined are those between (*1*) fixity and freedom, (*2*) law and love, and (*3*) authority and experience. On the one hand, there are those who stress the need for structure and stability if the social order is to be maintained. Aware of the precarious nature of our moral balance and the difficulty of the struggle to produce tolerable harmonies of justice among men, the defenders of fixity and authority attach a high value to the corporate wisdom of the past as it has become enshrined in the network of customs, conventions, and working rules that guide civilized behavior. Conscious of the thinness of the veneer of self-control that separates civilization from barbarism, they urge the need for discipline and self-restraint in the Christian life, and insist that if a man is to hear the gospel as good news, he must first take the law with the utmost seriousness. The presumption is that the provisions of the Christian moral tradition inherited from the past are generally valid today, and are to be departed from only after the gravest moral consideration and counsel, if at all. Defenders of such a position can point to the fallen character of human nature and to the innumerable specific moral precepts to be found in the New Testament. They rightly point out that the vast majority of men are unlikely to reach sound moral judgments without authoritative moral guidance, and believe that it is the Church's duty to provide such guidance, whether men heed it or not. On the other hand, those stressing the need for freedom and the sovereignty of love are keenly aware of the danger of legalism inherent in the traditionalist approach and are sensitive to, and sharply critical of, the moral pretensions of the self-righteous. They know that many a person keeps himself unspotted from the world out of sheer timidity and the steady pressures of conformity.[28] Although agreed upon the need for structure in the social order and for personal restraint and discipline, they emphasize the freedom and spontaneity of that love which is the fulfillment of all law. They are content to trust love's instinct to do what is needed in the specific situation, and are suspicious of premature efforts to restrict love to patterns which derive from social conventions and custom rather than from the New Testament and the demands of the specific situation. They rightly stress that a servile obedience, although it may satisfy the demands of conventional morality and conformity, is far from the filial obedience which the New Testament commends, and, furthermore, leads to spiritual or emotional breakdown and despair.

Although this writer is broadly sympathetic with the advocates of the "new morality" and agrees that it is scarcely new,[29] it does seem clear that so far, at least, its proponents have not given sufficient attention to the frailty of human nature and have not been sufficiently explicit as to the place of restraint, discipline, and law itself in the life of grace.[30] The struggle against rigorism and legalism is a perennial struggle in the Church's life, and the vigor with which the attack is being pressed just now is an altogether healthy sign. At the same time, it is important for the new moralists to bear in mind that what is required now and always is an ethic for men and not angels. Possibly because they are themselves devout churchmen, the newer moralists do not seem sufficiently aware that many do not share the years of practice of the Christian life as a daily discipline which, for a man like Dr. Robinson, are as much a part of experience as the rising and setting of the sun. One has the uneasy feeling that much which has so far been written implies an unduly optimistic view of human nature that neither sound biblical scholarship nor the Christian tradition, let alone empirical observation, would support.[31] There is need to make explicit a great deal which so far, at least, has been implied or presupposed about the nature of man and the need for discipline and guidance if man is to use his freedom in Christ for Christian ends. Dr. Robinson is right in his contention that the "new morality" needs certain emphases and insights which the "old morality" should be in a position to provide. It will scarcely do so, however, unless it is prepared to forego the posture of blind and fanatical opposition which was one of the more unsavory features of much popular discussion during 1963-64. There is room for creative dialogue in the field of Christian morals. The challenge has been thrown down, as it were, by the advocates of the "new morality." It must be taken up if the discussion is to move forward along genuinely constructive lines. Should that take place, and one sincerely hopes it will, there is no assurance that the results of sound discussion of the principles and practice of the Christian life can or will be translated into an effective social witness on the part of the Church.

There is evidence that the discussion is getting down to some of the fundamental questions for Christian morals and that they are being discussed with a frankness and realism which has not been evident in the recent past. There are other encouraging signs. One is the growing awareness of the close relationship between immorality, or what has been so regarded, and pathology. This awareness has made the consideration of such problems as alcoholism, drug addiction, and homosexuality both more enlightened and humane. In the area of sexual and marital relations, young persons today have a real and accurate knowledge of human biology and its importance for personal relationships. Increasingly, sexual intercourse is understood as the deepest expression of mutual need, respect, and love, rather than the casual satisfaction of physical desire on the part of two persons who may care nothing for each other. "If the former type of sexual expression is increasing, as it seems to be," writes Harry C. Meserve, "while the latter decreases, can we really say that this is a moral corruption, even if it occurs before marriage? Rather, it may be an evidence of a sincere search for personal integrity, sincerity, and responsibility." [32] The witness of the American Negro and his white allies in the nonviolent struggle for civil rights has stirred the conscience of a nation, however much remains to be done to win the struggle for justice and equality of opportunity for the Negro and other minority groups in the United States. The enthusiastic and dedicated response of American youth to the Peace Corps scarcely indicates widespread moral decadence. Moral vitality as well as moral decadence is a challenge to moral codes inherited from the past, and it is important not to confuse the two. The present situation is very much in a state of flux and offers unusual opportunities as well as dangers. Only time will tell whether the Church will be able to seize the opportunities and speak meaningfully to the needs of the present generation for realistic and humane moral ideals and standards.

Epilogue

A SURVEY written so close to the period in question must be only an interim report. I am keenly aware of areas and of authors sorely neglected in the kind of survey undertaken in the preceding pages. In the past quarter-century, doctrinal theology has not occupied the center of attention; the most constructive work has been done elsewhere. It seems clear that Anglican theology has reached another turning point. The fervor attached to biblical theology, liturgical renewal, and even the ecumenical movement has to a considerable extent run its course. But concern for these matters will continue to absorb the minds and zeal of many within the Church. Their long-range effect is impossible to evaluate. The jury is still out and must remain out for some time to come. Other concerns such as the mission and ministry of the laity, natural theology, and the renewed discussion of Christian ethics and moral theology are moving to the center of attention. It seems likely that Anglican theology will continue to make its contribution in each of these areas, increasingly in cooperation with other traditions. It will, in all likelihood, become more difficult to speak of a distinctive Anglican theology. This is cause for rejoicing rather than dismay, for it has always been the claim of Anglicans that there is no Anglican theology in the sense of a body of doctrine which belongs to that communion and not to the Church as a whole. Because of their tradition of sound and godly learning, with its insistence on seeking the truth, wherever the quest may lead and whatever the cost to cherished opinions from the past, Anglican theologians are particularly well suited to make their contribution in an age of profound and increasing religious unsettlement. The future of the Church, as well as the various portions thereof, remains in God's hands. Only he can determine to what extent it is to be a fit instrument of his purposes. Our task is to heed the stirrings of the Spirit wherever they may be discerned, and to strive as best we can to stand on God's side, devoting ourselves to those causes that we believe to be his, in this his world.

Author's Notes

Author's Notes

Introduction

1. For the period 1889-1939, A. M. Ramsey, *An Era of Anglican Theology* (New York: Scribner, 1960), is the most comprehensive survey. L. E. Elliott-Binns, *English Thought—1860-1900: The Theological Aspect* (New York: Seabury, 1956), deals with the background out of which *Lux Mundi* (London: Murray, 1890) emerged. Walter Horton, *Contemporary English Theology* (New York: Harper & Row, 1936), surveys more-recent developments. Also useful are J. K. Mozley, *Some Tendencies in Recent British Theology* (London: Macmillan, 1951), and H. D. A. Major, *English Modernism* (Cambridge, Mass.: Harvard University Press, 1927). G. L. Prestige, *The Life of Charles Gore* (London: Heinemann, 1935); F. A. Iremonger, *William Temple* (New York: Oxford, 1948); and G. K. A. Bell, *Randall Davidson* (London: Oxford, 1935), deal with the major personalities and events of the period. Helpful also is Roger Lloyd, *The Church of England in the 20th Century* (London: Longmans, Vol. 1, 1946, Vol. 2, 1950). James Carpenter, *Gore* (London: Faith, 1961), is the definitive study of Gore's theology. For Temple's theology, see Robert Craig, *Social Concern in the Thought of William Temple* (Naperville, Ill.: Allenson, 1963); Joseph Fletcher, *William Temple* (New York: Seabury, 1963); and Owen Thomas, *William Temple's Philosophy of Religion* (New York: Seabury, 1961).

2. Temple's own contribution in this area is his small but important *Christianity and the Social Order* (New York: Penguin, 1942). For the background of this side of Anglican thought, see M. B. Reckitt, *Maurice to Temple* (London: Faber & Faber, 1947), which contains a valuable bibliography.

3. Charles Gore, *Roman Catholic Claims* (London: Murray, 1892 ed.), p. xii.

Chapter 1: Thrust Toward a Critical Point

1. L. E. Elliott-Binns, *Religion in the Victorian Era* (London: Lutterworth, 1936), pp. 131-132.

2. The Advertisement to the *Analogy* (London: 1736).

3. See David L. Edwards, "A New Stirring in English Christianity," *The Honest to God Debate* (Philadelphia: Westminster, 1963), pp. 13 ff.

4. Leslie Paul, *The Deployment and Payment of the Clergy* (London: Church Information Office, 1964), p. 11.

5. Charles Gore, *The Reconstruction of Belief* (New York: Scribner, 1926), Chap. 1 and *passim*.

6. J. V. Langmead Casserley, *The Retreat from Christianity in the Modern World* (London: Longmans, 1952).

7. *Ibid.,* Chap. 6, and E. R. Wickham, *Church and People in an Industrial City* (London: Lutterworth, 1957).

8. C. F. G. Masterman, *The Condition of England* (London: 1909), pp. 268 f., cited by E. R. Wickham, *op. cit.,* pp. 179 f.

9. Erich Meissner, *Germany in Peril* (London: Oxford, 1942), p. 37, cited by Alec R. Vidler, *Essays in Liberality* (London: SCM, 1957), p. 19.

10. *The Tablet,* July 26, 1947, cited by Vidler, *op. cit.,* p. 19.

11. E. R. Wickham, *op. cit.,* p. 205.

12. *Cf.* Leslie Paul, *op. cit.,* Chaps. 3, 4, 5.

13. Trevor Huddleston, *Naught for Your Comfort* (Garden City, N.Y.: Doubleday, 1956).

14. Ernest Southcott, *The Parish Comes Alive* (London: Mowbray, 1956), and J. A. T. Robinson, *On Being the Church in the World* (Philadelphia: Westminster, 1960), Chap. 5.

15. Howard A. Johnson, *Global Odyssey* (New York: Harper & Row, 1963), pp. 143 ff.

16. Martin Thornton, *Pastoral Theology: A Reorientation* (New York: Seabury, 1961), *Christian Proficiency* (New York: Morehouse-Barlow, 1959), *Feed My Lambs: Essays in Pastoral Reconstruction* (New York: Seabury, 1961).

17. A. Michael Ramsey, *Image Old and New* (London: SPCK, 1963), p. 14.

18. Samuel J. Wylie, *Precede the Dawn* (New York: Morehouse-Barlow, 1963), pp. 9 ff.

19. Gibson Winter, *The Suburban Captivity of the Churches* (Garden City, N.Y.: Doubleday, 1961), and *The New Creation as Metropolis* (Garden City, N.Y.: Doubleday, 1963).

20. *Christians in a Technological Era,* ed. by Hugh White (New York: Seabury, 1964).

21. *On the Battle Lines,* ed. by Malcolm Boyd (New York: Morehouse-Barlow, 1964).

22. Pierre Berton, *The Comfortable Pew* (Philadelphia: Lippincott, 1965), and Ernest Harrison, *Let God Go Free* (New York: Seabury, 1965).

23. Howard A. Johnson, *op. cit., passim.*

24. *Mutual Responsibility and Interdependence in the Body of Christ,* ed. by Stephen F. Bayne, Jr. (New York: Seabury, 1963), and Peter Whiteley, *Frontier Mission* (New York: Seabury, 1963). See also Stephen F. Bayne, Jr., *An Anglican Turning Point* (Austin, Tex.: Church Historical Society, 1964); Albert Theodore Eastman, *Christian Responsibility in One World* (New York: Seabury, 1965); Stephen Neill, *A History of Christian Missions* (Baltimore, Md.: Penguin, 1964); John V. Taylor, *Processes of Growth in an African Church* (London: SCM, 1958); *The Primal Vision* (London: SCM, 1963); Max Warren, *Perspective in Mission* (New York: Seabury, 1964), and *The Missionary Movement from Britain in Modern History* (London: SCM, 1965); Douglas Webster, *Mission and the New Theology* (London: *Prism* Pamphlet 21, 1965), and *Mutual Irresponsibility* (London: SPCK, 1965).

25. E. L. Mascall, *Christ, the Christian, and the Church* (London: Longmans, 1946), *Corpus Christi* (London: Longmans, 1953), *Via Media* (New York: Seabury, 1957), *The Importance of Being Human* (New York: Columbia University Press, 1958), *The Recovery of Unity* (London: Longmans, 1958).

Some of Austin Farrer's work in doctrinal theology is to be found in the pages of his biblical studies such as *A Rebirth of Images* (London: Dacre, 1949) and *A Study in St. Mark* (London: Dacre, 1951). More clearly doctrinal are his *The Glass of Vision* (London: Dacre, 1948), *The Freedom of the Will* (London: Black, 1958), *Love Almighty and Ills Unlimited* (Garden City, N.Y.: Doubleday, 1961), and *Saving Belief* (London: Hodder & Stoughton, 1964). In a more popular vein is *Lord, I Believe* (London: Faith, 1958).

Leonard Hodgson's more important doctrinal works are *The Doctrine of the Trinity* (New York: Scribner, 1944), *The Doctrine of the Atonement* (New York: Scribner, 1957), and *For Faith and Freedom* (New York: Scribner, 1957).

F. W. Dillistone has contributed *The Holy Spirit in the Life of Today* (Philadelphia: Westminster, 1947), *Jesus Christ and His Cross* (Philadelphia: Westminster, 1953), together with two major books on the Church and Sacraments: *The Structure of the Divine Society* (Philadelphia: Westminster, 1951) and *Christianity and Symbolism* (Philadelphia: Westminster, 1955). In a more popular vein is his *The Christian Faith* (London: Hodder & Stoughton, 1964).

Of the many books of W. Norman Pittenger, the more important are *Christ and the Christian Message* (New York: Round Table, 1941), *Theology and Reality* (New York: Seabury, 1955), *Rethinking the Christian Message* (New York: Seabury, 1956), and *The Church, the Ministry, and Reunion* (New York: Seabury, 1957). His book on the Eucharist is *The Christian Sacrifice* (New York: Oxford, 1951). *The Word Incarnate* (New York: Harper & Row, 1959) is an important study of Christology.

William Wolf has written two doctrinal studies, *Man's Knowledge of God* (Garden City, N.Y.: Doubleday, 1955), and *No Cross, No Crown* (Garden City, N.Y.: Doubleday, 1957), which is an important study of the Atonement.

Arthur A. Vogel's books are *Reality, Reason, and Religion* (New York: Morehouse-Barlow, 1957) and *The Christian Person* (New York: Seabury, 1963).

26. *The Church in the Sixties,* ed. by P. C. Jefferson (New York: Seabury, 1962).

27. *Soundings,* ed. by Alec R. Vidler (New York: Cambridge, 1962), p. ix.

28. *Theology,* Nov., 1939.

29. *Theology,* Jan., 1960, p. 2.

30. E. R. Wickham, *op. cit.,* p. 193.

Chapter 2: Not Finality but Direction

1. *Biblical Authority for Today,* ed. by Alan Richardson and W. Schweitzer (Philadelphia: Westminster, 1952), pp. 112 f.

2. Stephen Neill, *Anglicanism* (Baltimore, Md.: Penguin, 1960), p. 418.

3. *Modern Canterbury Pilgrims,* ed. by James A. Pike (New York: Morehouse-Barlow, 1956), p. 98.

4. See the proposals for post-ordination training made by Leslie Paul, *The Deployment and Payment of the Clergy* (London: Church Information Office, 1964), pp. 210 ff. The College of Preachers, Washington, D.C.; the Institute for Advanced Pastoral Training, Bloomfield Hills, Mich.; and the programs of the Council for Clinical Training, 475 Riverside Drive, New York, N. Y. 10027, provide indications of the sort of greatly expanded opportunities for post-ordination training which are needed.

5. *Essays in Liberality* (London: SCM, 1957), p. 38.

6. Cited by Alan Richardson, *op. cit.,* p. 114.

7. *Ibid.,* p. 114.

8. See the discussion in E. J. Bicknell, *A Theological Introduction to the Thirty-nine Articles* (London: Longmans, 1955 ed.), pp. 17 ff. Recent proposals for revision of the Articles to bring them in line with the present belief and practice of the Church of England include W. R. Matthews, *The Thirty-nine Articles* (London: Hodder & Stoughton, 1961), and C. B. Moss, *The Thirty-nine Articles Revised* (London: Mowbray, 1961).

9. In discussion with priest-students at St. Augustine's College, Canterbury, in Dec., 1962.

10. Alan Richardson, *op. cit.,* p. 113.

11. See the Preface of the American Book of Common Prayer; Richard Hooker, *Of the Laws of Ecclesiastical Polity,* esp. Bk. III; Matt. 16: 18-19; and Charles Gore, *The Reconstruction of Belief* (New York: Scribner, 1926), pp. 763 f.

12. *Anglicanism,* ed. by Paul Elmer More and F. L. Cross (New York: Morehouse-Barlow, 1935), p. xxv.

13. The American Book of Common Prayer, pp. 533, 542, 554, *cf.* Article VIII; E. A. White and J. A. Dykman, *Annotated Constitution and Canons for the Government of the Protestant Episcopal Church* (New York: Seabury, 1954), pp. 102 ff.

14. *Cf.* J. H. Newman, *The Development of Christian Doctrine* (New York: Appleton, 1845), with the reply by J. B. Mozley, *Theory of Development* (London: Oxford, 1847), and Charles Gore, *op. cit.,* pp. 828 ff.

15. *Documents of the Christian Church,* ed. by Henry Bettenson (New York: Oxford, 1947), pp. 442-445.

16. Article VIII of the Thirty-nine Articles. For a summary of discussion concerning the authority of the creeds, see A. M. Ramsey, *An Era of Anglican Theology* (New York: Scribner, 1960), Chap. 6. The adequacy of the creeds to summarize Christian faith for modern man has recently been questioned by James A. Pike, *A Time for Christian Candor* (New York: Harper & Row, 1964), and J. A. T. Robinson, *The New Reformation?* (Philadelphia: Westminster, 1965), Chaps. 2 and 4.

17. Several recent examples are John Burnaby, *The Belief of Christendom* (London: SPCK, 1960); *Mirfield Essays in Christian Belief,* ed. by Martin Jarrett-Kerr (New York: Morehouse-Barlow, 1963); F. W. Dillistone, *The Christian Faith* (London: Hodder & Stoughton, 1964); and Austin Farrer, *Saving Belief* (London: Hodder & Stoughton, 1964).

18. *Anglicanism,* p. xxviii.

19. *Ibid.,* p. xxii.

20. E. L. Mascall, *Via Media* (New York: Seabury, 1957), the Foreword and *passim.*

21. *Anglicanism,* p. xxviii. *Cf.* with William Temple, *Nature, Man, and God* (London: Macmillan, 1935), p. 353.

22. James A. Pike, *A Time for Christian Candor,* p. 23.

23. Paul Elmer More, *op. cit.,* pp. xx ff.

24. J. K. Mozley, *Some Tendencies in Recent British Theology* (London: Macmillan, 1951), pp. 83-87.

25. William Temple, *Nature, Man, and God,* and *Christus Veritas* (London: Macmillan, 1950). For an exhaustive bibliography of Temple's writings, together with a biographical sketch and an admirable interpretative study, see Joseph Fletcher, *William Temple* (New York: Seabury, 1963).

The best introduction to F. D. Maurice is Alec R. Vidler, *Witness to the Light* (New York: Scribner, 1948); the English title is *The Theology of F. D. Maurice. Toward the Recovery of Unity,* ed. by John F. Porter and William J. Wolf (New York: Seabury, 1964), is a selection of Maurice's letters, together with an introductory essay. Maurice's *The Kingdom of Christ* (London: SCM, 1958, based on 2nd ed. of 1842) has been republished, as has his *Theological Essays* (New York: Harper & Row, 1957).

Interpretative studies of Maurice are A. M. Ramsey, *F. D. Maurice and the Conflicts of Modern Theology* (London: Cambridge, 1951); H. G. Wood, *Frederick Denison Maurice* (London: Cambridge, 1950); and Ian T. Ramsey, *On Being Sure in Religion* (New York: Oxford, 1963).

26. William Temple, *op. cit.,* pp. 312, 317, 322.

27. A. M. Ramsey, *An Era of Anglican Theology,* p. 91.

28. *Soundings,* ed. by Alec R. Vidler (New York: Cambridge University Press, 1962), p. 145.

29. Charles Gore, *Can We Then Believe?* (London: Murray, 1926), pp. 149 f.

30. *Ibid.,* p. 151.

31. *Anglicanism,* p. xxxiv.

32. Ian T. Ramsey, *Religious Language* (Naperville, Ill.: Allenson, 1957), Chap. 1, and *On Being Sure in Religion.*

33. In *Northern Catholicism* (New York: Macmillan, 1933), p. 233.

34. Paul Elmer More in *Anglicanism,* p. xxii.

Chapter 3: Toward Deeper Foundations: Biblical Theology

1. Alan Richardson, *The Bible in the Age of Science* (Philadelphia: Westminster, 1961), and Stephen Neill, *The Interpretation of the New Testament 1861-1961* (New York: Oxford, 1964), provide surveys of the development of biblical studies during the last century. For more recent

developments, see also Reginald H. Fuller, *The New Testament in Current Study* (New York: Scribner, 1962).

2. A. M. Ramsey, *An Era of Anglican Theology* (New York: Scribner, 1960), Chap. 9.

3. Karl Barth, *The Epistle to the Romans,* trans. by E. C. Hoskyns (New York: Oxford, 1933), Preface, p. 11.

4. The series "Studies in Biblical Theology" (London: SCM) is illustrative of the caliber of work being done.

5. For further discussion of Hoskyns and his influence, see A. M. Ramsey, *op. cit.,* pp. 129-145; Roger Lloyd, *The Church of England in the Twentieth Century* (London: Longmans, 1950), Vol. 2, pp. 48 ff.; *The Church Quarterly Review,* July-Sept., 1957, pp. 280-295, and July-Sept., 1958, pp. 325-340.

6. A. M. Hunter, *Interpreting the New Testament 1900-1950* (Philadelphia: Westminster, 1952), p. 127.

7. See note 1. above. Particularly outstanding in recent decades has been the work of R. H. Lightfoot, Charles F. D. Moule, and David Nineham in England, and, in the United States, that of Frederick C. Grant and John Knox. For an evaluation of the many-sided work of Lionel Thornton, see A. M. Ramsey, *Canterbury Essays and Addresses* (New York: Seabury, 1964), pp. 127-132.

8. A. G. Hebert, *The Bible from Within* (London: Oxford, 1950), p. 3.

9. *Ibid.,* p. 5.

10. *Scripture and the Faith* (New York: Morehouse-Barlow, 1962); *The Bible from Within; When Israel Came Out of Egypt* (Richmond, Va.: John Knox, 1961).

11. *An Era of Anglican Theology* and *Canterbury Essays and Addresses,* particularly the essays in Sec. 4, pp. 107 ff.

12. *The Glory of God and the Transfiguration of Christ* (London: Longmans, 1949), p. 6.

13. "The Authority of the Bible," *Peake's Commentary on the Bible* (New York: Nelson, 1962); *Durham Essays and Addresses* (London: SPCK, 1956), pp. 22-35; and *The Narratives of the Passion* (Westminster, Md.: Canterbury, 1962).

14. *Theology,* Jan., 1959, p. 1.

15. *Introduction to the Theology of the New Testament* (New York: Harper & Row, 1959), p. 12.

16. *The Bible in the Age of Science,* p. 78.

17. *Ibid.,* p. 149. See Ronald Hepburn's criticisms of the argument of *Christian Apologetics* in *Christianity and Paradox* (New York: Humanities, 1956), pp. 112 ff.

18. E.g., Alan Richardson, *The Bible in the Age of Science,* p. 149.

19. See, e.g., Ninian Smart in *Soundings,* pp. 105 ff., and Ian T. Ramsey, *Religious Language* (Naperville, Ill.: Allenson, 1957), pp. 103 ff.

Chapter 4: The Promise of Liturgical Renewal

1. Louis Bouyer, *Liturgical Piety,* (Notre Dame, Ind.: University of Notre Dame Press, 1955); the English title is *Life and Liturgy* (London: Sheed & Ward, 1956); J. D. Benoit, *Liturgical Renewal* [Studies in Catholic and Protestant Developments on the Continent] (London: SCM, 1958).

2. See, however, *The Parish Communion Today,* ed. by David M. Paton (London: SPCK, 1963), pp. 1-12; *The Parish Communion,* ed. by A. G. Hebert (London: SPCK, 1937); *The Liturgical Renewal of the Church,* ed. by Massey H. Shepherd, Jr. (New York: Oxford, 1960), pp. 21-52; and Massey H. Shepherd, Jr., *The Reform of Liturgical Worship* (New York: Oxford, 1961).

3. "What the Anglo-Catholic of a hundred years ago was able to borrow from the Catholics of the time were precisely those features which now appear to Catholics to be among the weakest points in their liturgical practice. For example, a preference for low mass (as private as possible) rather than a public celebration; the high mass itself carried out so as to do without communion or any participation by the faithful; and, above all, an enthusiasm for the Benediction of the Blessed Sacrament which tended to make it, rather than the Mass itself, the focus of congregational worship." Louis Bouyer, *op. cit.,* p. 48.

4. *The Reform of Liturgical Worship,* pp. 11-33.

5. Massey H. Shepherd, Jr., *The Liturgical Movement and the Prayer Book* (Evanston, Ill.: Seabury-Western Theological Seminary, 1946), pp. 10 ff.

6. See, e.g., the series "Ecumenical Studies in Worship" (Richmond, Va.: John Knox Press) and "Studies in Ministry and Worship" (London: SCM). The journal *Studia Liturgica* is "An International and Ecumenical Quarterly for Liturgical Research and Renewal." *Worship in Scripture and Tradition* (New York: Oxford, 1963) contains essays by members of the Theological Commission on Worship (North American Section) of the Commission on Faith and Order of the World Council of Churches.

7. The texts are found in *The Liturgy in English,* ed. by Bernard Wigan (New York: Oxford, 1962).

8. Pub. by The Church Pension Fund, 20 Exchange Place, New York, N.Y., in 16 (paperbound) vols.

9. *The Reform of Liturgical Worship,* pp. 114, 95-114, where the proposal is fully set forth.

10. *The Liturgical Renewal of the Church* (1960); *The Reform of Liturgical Worship* (1961); *Liturgy Is Mission,* ed. by Frank S. Cellier (New York: Seabury, 1964). A similar volume of essays is *Living Thankfully,* ed. by Harold R. Landon (New York: Seabury, 1961).

11. G. W. O. Addleshaw and Frederick Etchells, *The Architectural Setting of Anglican Worship* (London: Faber & Faber, 1948); Basil Spence, *Phoenix at Coventry* (London: Bles, 1962); Peter Hammond, *Liturgy and Architecture* (London: Barrie & Rockliff, 1960); *Making the Building Serve the Liturgy,* ed. by Gilbert Cope (London: Mowbray, 1962).

12. *Theology,* Nov., 1960, p. 451.

13. A. G. Hebert, *Liturgy and Society* (London: Faber & Faber, 1935), p. 8.

14. *Ibid.,* pp. 9 f.

15. *The Parish Communion,* p. v.

16. *Ibid.,* p. viii.

17. Dom Gregory Dix, *The Shape of the Liturgy* (London: Dacre, 1945), p. xviii.

18. In *Theology,* Nov., 1960, p. 452.

19. *Ibid.,* p. 4.

20. Alan Paton, "Meditation, For a Young Boy Confirmed," *Holy Communion,* ed. by Massey H. Shepherd, Jr. (New York: Seabury, 1959), pp. 149-150.

21. Kenneth E. Kirk, *The Vision of God,* abr. ed. (London: Longmans, 1934), pp. 191, 186.

22. See Chap. 1, *supra,* esp. p. 24.

23. Samuel J. Wylie, *Precede the Dawn* (New York: Morehouse-Barlow, 1963), Chap. 2.

24. A. M. Ramsey, *Durham Essays and Addresses* (London: SPCK, 1956), pp. 15-22; E. L. Mascall, *The Recovery of Unity* (London: Longmans, 1958), pp. 142 f; Henry de Candole in *The Parish Communion Today,* pp. 8 f.

Chapter 5: The Hesitant Quest for Unity

1. Ruth Rowse and Stephen Neill, *A History of the Ecumenical Movement* (Philadelphia: Westminster, 1954); Georges Henri Tavard, *Two*

Centuries of Ecumenism, trans. by Roger Hughes (Notre Dame, Ind.: University of Notre Dame Press, 1960); *Documents on Christian Unity,* ed. by G. K. A. Bell, Ser. 1-4 (London: Oxford, 1924-1958).

2. See A. M. Ramsey, *An Era of Anglican Theology* (New York: Scribner, 1960), Chap. 8, for a summary of the discussion down to Temple's death. E. R. Fairweather and R. F. Hettlinger, *Episcopacy and Reunion* (London: Mowbray, 1953), provides an admirable summary of the several views within Anglican theology on the question. E. L. Mascall, *The Recovery of Unity* (London: Longmans, 1958), is a survey of the discussion from an Anglo-Catholic perspective down to 1958.

3. *Documents of the Christian Church,* ed. by Henry Bettenson (New York: Oxford, 1947), pp. 442 f.

4. *Catholicity—A Study in the Conflict of Christian Traditions in the West* (London: Dacre, 1947), pp. 44 f. A comparable report prepared by Anglican Evangelicals is *The Fullness of Christ* (London: SPCK, 1950).

5. *Ibid.,* p. 45.

6. Fr. Gregory Baum writes: ". . . it is only in recent times that the official documents of the Holy See have been ready to admit that the divisions of Christendom actually do harm to the Catholic Church, and that the whole Mystical Body will benefit from the perfect reconciliation of Christians. In former times the benefits of a reunion were foreseen only for the Separated Churches. However, Pius XI and Pius XII are quite outspoken; they look forward also to the wholesome effects of Christian unity on the Catholic Church. 'From the full and perfect unity of all Christians the Mystical Body of Christ and all its members, one by one, are bound to obtain great increment.' " Quoted in *An American Dialogue,* by Robert Brown and Gustave Weigel, S.J. (Garden City, N.Y.: Doubleday, 1961).

7. *Essays in Anglican Self-Criticism* (London: SCM, 1958), pp. 174 f.

8. For recent ecumenical statements of faith, see especially the reports of the ecumenical conferences held at Lausanne (1927), Jerusalem (1928), Edinburgh (1937), Tambaram (1938), Amsterdam (1948), Evanston (1954), and New Delhi (1961).

9. In *Steps Toward Unity* (London: Mowbray, 1919), pamphlet, p. 5.

10. *The Lambeth Conference* (New York: Seabury, 1958), *cf.* Sec. 2, pp. 24 ff.

11. *Ceylon, North India, Pakistan* (A Study in Ecumenical Decision), ed. by Stephen F. Bayne, Jr. (London: SPCK, 1960); *Conversations* [Between the Church of England and the Methodist Church: A Report] (London: Church Information Office, 1963); David M. Paton, *One Church Renewed for Mission* (London: SCM, 1964).

12. See the official reports of the Lambeth conferences of 1948 and 1958.

13. See that portion of the Appeal quoted *supra*.

14. *The Apostolic Ministry*, ed. by Kenneth E. Kirk (New York: Morehouse-Barlow, 1947), p. 8.

15. *Ibid.*, p. 23.

16. *Ibid.*, p. 303.

17. Kenneth E. Kirk, *ibid.*, pp. 23-24.

18. *Ibid.*, p. 40.

19. For detailed criticism, see Stephen Neill and others, *The Ministry of the Church* (London: Canterbury, 1947); T. W. Manson, *The Church's Ministry* (London: Hodder & Stoughton, 1948); A. E. J. Rawlinson, *Problems of Reunion* (London: Eyre & Spottiswood, 1950); and R. F. Hettlinger in *Episcopacy and Reunion*, pp. 63 ff.

20. Austin Farrer in the Preface to the 2nd ed. of *The Apostolic Ministry* (pub. sep. by the Church Union Church Literature Association, 1957).

21. *Cf.*: "Every link in the chain is known, from S. Peter to our present Metropolitans. Here then I only ask, looking at the plain fact by itself, is there not something of a divine providence in it? Can we conceive that this succession has been preserved, all over the world, amid many revolutions, through many centuries, for nothing?" (J. H. Newman in Tract 7) with the treatment of succession by Charles Gore, *The Church and the Ministry* (London: Longmans, 1936 ed.) and *Orders and Unity* (New York: Dutton, 1909), and by A. M. Ramsey, *The Gospel and the Catholic Church* (London: Longmans, 1956 ed.), esp. Chap. 6.

22. J. E. L. Newbigin, *The Reunion of the Church* (London: SCM, 1948), p. 56 and *cf.* pp. 108-109.

23. "It is quite true that the Church of England imposes upon the clergy no obligation to hold the dogma that only Episcopal ordinations are valid, and only priestly consecrations of the eucharist, and that bishops are of the esse of the Church, but it has acted, so far as its corporate action, always in such a way as to satisfy those who hold these doctrines, and to impose severe restrictions on the action of those who do not hold them would naturally wish to take." Charles Gore in *The Basis of Anglican Fellowship* (London: Mowbray, 1914), p. 34. See also G. W. H. Lampe, *An Anglican Approach to Intercommunion and Reunion* (London: SPCK, 1962), p. 17.

24. J. A. T. Robinson in *The Historic Episcopate*, ed. by Kenneth M. Carey (London: Dacre, 1954), pp. 22 f.

25. In *Unity and Schism* (London: Mowbray, 1917). See the discussion by A. M. Ramsey, *An Era in Anglican Theology*, pp. 122 f.

26. "I utterly believe that the four strands—Scripture, Creeds, Sacraments, episcopal ministry—are essential strands in the union of the Christian or Branch with the Body of Christ or the True Vine. But if a Branch is partly severed, it still lives with the life of the tree. It suffers from the lack of the form of connection that is lost; it lives by what is left, and is still a part of the tree. . . . I could only agree that all future ordinations are episcopal. But, if that is agreed, I would go far in recognizing the *de facto* efficacy of the existing ministries. And I would greatly respect the concern of Free Churchmen lest in accepting (re)ordination they should in fact strengthen the hold of the vicious theory which has grown out of Augustine's handling of the Donatists." William Temple in a letter to A. M. Ramsey, cited by Ramsey, *op. cit.,* pp. 124 f.

27. Norman Sykes, *Old Priest and New Presbyter* (New York: Cambridge, 1956), p. 261. *Cf.* the discussion in E. L. Mascall, *The Recovery of Unity,* pp. 163 f., which is critical of Sykes's views.

28. *Cf.* the discussion of St. Augustine by R. F. Hettlinger, *op. cit.,* pp. 82 f., and by A. G. Hebert, *Apostle and Bishop* (New York: Seabury, 1963), Chap. 4.

29. A. M. Ramsey, *The Gospel and the Catholic Church,* Chap. 6.

30. See, e.g., Daniel T. Jenkins, *The Nature of Catholicity* (London: Faber & Faber, 1943), and A. G. Hebert, *The Form of the Church* (London: Faber & Faber, 1944).

31. *Essays in Anglican Self-Criticism,* p. 196.

32. William Temple, *The Church Looks Forward* (London: Macmillan, 1944), p. 25, cited by A. M. Ramsey, *An Era of Anglican Theology,* pp. 125 f.

Chapter 6: Ministry and Mission

1. E. L. Mascall, "Anglican Dogmatic Theology, 1939-1960," *Theology,* Jan., 1960, *cf.* pp. 4 f. See also A. M. Ramsey, *An Era of Anglican Theology* (New York: Scribner, 1960), Chaps. 8 and 10.

2. H. P. Liddon, *Life of Edward Bouverie Pusey* (London: Longmans, 1893), Vol. I, p. 238, cited by Alec R. Vidler, *Essays in Liberality* (London: SCM, 1957), pp. 155 f.

3. *Laity,* bulletin of the Department on the Laity of the World Council of Churches, Geneva, Switzerland; *Evanston Speaks,* report of the Second Assembly of the World Council of Churches, 1954, *cf.* Sec. VI: "The Laity —The Christian in His Vocation"; Hendrik Kraemer, *A Theology of the Laity* (Philadelphia: Westminster, 1958); Y. M. J. Congar, *Lay People in the Church* (London: Bloomsbury, 1957); Howard Grimes, *The Rebirth of the Laity* (New York: Abingdon, 1962); Georgia Harkness, *The Church and Its Laity* (New York: Abingdon, 1963); Alden D. Kelley, *The People*

of God (New York: Seabury, 1962); Arnold B. Come, *Agents of Reconcili-ation* (Philadelphia: Westminster, 1963).

4. G. Michonneau, *Revolution in a City Parish,* Eng. trans. (London: Blackfriars, 1949); J. de Blank, *The Parish in Action* (London: Mowbray, 1954); T. Allen, *The Face of My Parish* (London: SCM, 1954); E. W. Southcott, *The Parish Comes Alive* (London: Mowbray, 1956); M. Hock-ing, *The Parish Seeks a Way* (London: Mowbray, 1960); T. Beeson, *New Area Mission* (London: Mowbray, 1963); R. A. Raines, *New Life in the Church* (New York: Harper & Row, 1961); R. A. Raines, *Reshaping the Christian Life* (New York: Harper & Row, 1964); *On the Battle Lines,* ed. by Malcolm Boyd (New York: Morehouse-Barlow, 1963).

5. Maisie Ward, *France Pagan?* (London: Sheed & Ward, 1950); E. R. Wickham, *Church and People in an Industrial City* (London: Lutterworth, 1957); Colin W. Williams, *Where in the World?* and *What in the World?* (New York: National Council of Churches, 475 Riverside Drive, 1963 and 1964).

6. E. R. Wickham, *op. cit.,* Chap. 6.

7. Gibson Winter, *The New Creation as Metropolis* (Garden City, N.Y.: Doubleday, 1963).

8. Gibson Winter, *The Suburban Captivity of the Churches* (Garden City, N.Y.: Doubleday, 1961).

9. *Sword and Shield,* Bulletin of the Parishfield Community, Brighton, Mich., Feb.-Mar., 1964.

10. *Centres of Renewal* (World Council of Churches, Geneva, Switz-erland, 1964) and Olive Wyon, *Living Springs* (London: SCM, 1963).

11. *Cf.* Leslie Paul, *The Deployment and Payment of the Clergy* (Lon-don: Church Information Office, 1964), and Chap. 1, *supra.*

12. Colin Williams, *Where in the World?, cf.* pp. 59 f.

13. F. R. Barry, *Vocation and Ministry* (London: Nisbet, 1958), and *Asking the Right Questions* (London: Hodder & Stoughton, 1960); H. Richard Niebuhr, Daniel D. Williams, and James M. Gustafson, *The Ad-vancement of Theological Education* (New York: Harper & Row, 1957). *Cf.* the chapter by James Gustafson on the "Ten Types of Men Entering the Ministry." Statistics on the number of men ordained each year may be found in *Crockford's Clerical Directory* and the *Episcopal Church Annual.*

14. David Riesman, *The Lonely Crowd* (New Haven, Conn.: Yale University Press, 1953).

15. Margaretta Bowers, *Conflicts of the Clergy* (New York: Nelson, 1963); Charles R. Stinnette, Jr., "The Church and Psychology," *Viewpoints,* ed. by John Coburn and W. Norman Pittenger (New York: Seabury, 1959), pp. 193 ff.

16. See *Syllabus for Theological Studies,* prepared by the Joint Commission on Theological Education, available from the Episcopal Church Center, 815 Second Ave., New York, N.Y. 10017.

17. To some extent, this is already the case through the efforts of diocesan departments of Christian Education and Christian Social Relations and the programs of the College of Preachers, Washington, D.C.; the School of Prophets, San Francisco, Calif.; and the Urban Training Center for Christian Mission, Chicago, Ill. What is needed is a greatly expanded program which would make available such opportunities on a continuing basis for all interested clergy.

18. Proposals for reform have been made in Leslie Paul's *The Deployment and Payment of the Clergy* and in Samuel J. Wylie's *Precede the Dawn* (New York: Morehouse-Barlow, 1963). The proposals are very much in the planning stage, however, and the natural conservatism of ecclesiastical organizations and their dogged defense of existing privilege and the status quo do not make one optimistic about their early implementation in an effective manner.

19. Mark Gibbs and T. Ralph Morton, *God's Frozen People* (Philadelphia: Westminster, 1964), *passim*.

20. Kathleen Bliss, *We the People* (Philadelphia: Fortress, 1964).

21. J. A. T. Robinson in *New Ways with the Ministry,* ed. by John Morris (London: Faith, 1960), pp. 9 ff.

22. Richard S. Emrich in *Part Time Priests?,* ed. by Robin Denniston (London: Skeffington, 1960), pp. 49 f., 55.

23. Alden D. Kelley, *The People of God,* Chap. 4; *New Ways with the Ministry,* pp. 18 ff.; *Prism,* Apr., 1964, pp. 36-38; *The Living Church,* May 2, 9, 16, (1965).

24. *The Layman in Christian History,* ed. by Stephen Neill and Hans-Ruedi Weber (Philadelphia: Westminster, 1963); Francis O. Ayres, *The Ministry of the Laity* (Philadelphia: Westminster, 1962); Alden D. Kelley, *op. cit.;* F. R. Barry, *Asking the Right Questions,* esp. pp. 82-90. Admirable brief surveys are those of Emma Lou Benignus in *Viewpoints,* pp. 109 ff.; and Hans-Ruedi Weber, *Salty Christians* (New York: Seabury, 1963).

25. *Priests and Workers,* ed. by David L. Edwards (London: SCM Press, 1961), esp. pp. 124 ff. John Rowe, *Priests and Workers: A Rejoinder* (London: Darton, Longman & Todd, 1965).

26. *Part Time Priests?,* ed. by Robin Denniston.

27. *Cf.* Michael Ramsey's essay in *Part Time Priests?,* pp. 24 ff.

28. *Bishops,* ed. by the Bishop of Llandaff (London: Faith, 1961).

29. Basil Minchin, *Every Man in His Ministry* (London: Darton, Longman & Todd, 1960), pp. 156-158, 180-194.

30. *Evanston 1954* (official report of the Second Assembly), pp. 104 f.

31. *Ibid.*, pp. 104 f.

32. *New Ways with the Ministry*, pp. 29, 31, 53.

33. Cited in *Salty Christians*, pp. 3 f.

34. Alec R. Vidler, *Essays in Liberality*, pp. 29 ff.

35. J. A. T. Robinson, *The New Reformation?* (Philadelphia: Westminster, 1965), p. 63.

36. "Every human being is stamped by his trade. His profession has chiselled his personality. It is his means of entering into communication with human striving, and it is nearly always the window or skylight that limits his view of the world. It is his contribution to the human effort to master nature. Most men's habits of thought and of reaction run in the mould of their work." J. M. Perrin in *Forward the Layman,* trans. by Katherine Gordon (London: Blackfriars, 1956), p. 126.

37. C. S. Lewis made effective use of allegory in his *Screwtape Letters* (New York: Macmillan, 1945) and in *The Great Divorce* (New York: Macmillan, 1946), as well as in his books for children such as *The Lion, the Witch, and the Wardrobe* (New York: Macmillan, 1950). Dorothy Sayers uses the analogy of the creative artist in her *Mind of the Maker* (New York: Harcourt, Brace & World, 1941) to throw light on the doctrines of Creation and the Trinity.

38. Monica Furlong, *With Love to the Church* (London: Hodder & Stoughton, 1965); D. L. Munby, *The Idea of a Secular Society* (New York: Oxford, 1963); John Wren-Lewis, *Faith, Fact, and Fantasy* (London: Collins, 1964); and the contributions of Mr. Munby and Mr. Wren-Lewis to *Essays in Anglican Self-Criticism,* ed. by David M. Paton (London: SCM, 1958).

Chapter 7: The Current Ferment

1. *The Honest to God Debate,* ed. by David L. Edwards (Philadelphia: Westminster, 1963), p. 7.

2. A. M. Ramsey, *Image Old and New* (London: SPCK, 1963), pamphlet; O. Fielding Clarke, *For Christ's Sake* (New York: Morehouse-Barlow, 1963); *Four Anchors from the Stern,* ed. by Alan Richardson (Naperville, Ill.: Allenson, 1963); J. I. Packer, *Keep Yourselves from Idols* (London: Church Book Room Press, 1963), pamphlet; Klaas Runia, *I Believe in God* (Chicago: Inter-Varsity, 1963); Roger Lloyd, *The Ferment in the Church* (New York: Morehouse-Barlow, 1964); John Burnaby, *Our Thought of God* (London: SPCK, 1964), pamphlet; A. M. Ramsey, *Beyond Religion?* (London: SPCK, 1964), pamphlet. *The Honest to God Debate* contains a broad selection of reviews. In addition, see *Prism,* Apr., 1963; *Theology,* Jan., 1964, pp. 1 f; *Scottish Journal of Theology,*

Sept., 1964, pp. 257-278. For some American reactions, see *Religion in Life,* Winter, 1964; *Christianity and Crisis,* Nov. 11, 1963; *The Christian Century,* pp. 603, 722, 1096 f.; and *Christianity Today,* Nov. 20, 1964,

Four books occasioned by *Honest to God* (Philadelphia: Westminster, 1963) which seek to carry the discussion further are: Erik Routley, *The Man for Others* (New York: Oxford, 1964); D. T. Niles, *We Know in Part* (Philadelphia: Westminster, 1964); Langdon Gilkey, *How the Church Can Minister to the World Without Losing Itself* (New York: Harper & Row, 1964); and James A. Pike, *A Time for Christian Candor* (New York: Harper & Row, 1964).

3. *The Honest to God Debate,* pp. 233 f.

4. See especially "Some Readers' Letters," *op. cit.,* pp. 48-81.

5. *The Times,* May 7, 1963.

6. *The Honest to God Debate,* p. 8.

7. *The Church Times,* Apr. 5, 1963.

8. *The Honest to God Debate,* p. 8.

9. For Dr. Robinson's account of the "publicity explosion," see *op. cit.,* pp. 233-241.

10. H. A. Williams in *The Times,* May 6, 1963.

11. *Cf.* with A. M. Ramsey, *Image Old and New* (London: SPCK, 1963), pp. 5, 14.

12. Monica Furlong in *The Guardian,* May 2, 1963.

13. *The Honest to God Debate,* p. 275.

14. *Prisoner for God: Letters and Papers from Prison* (New York: Macmillan, 1954), pp. 145 f., quoted in *Honest to God,* p. 36.

15. *The Observer,* Mar. 24, 1963.

16. *Encounter,* Sept., 1963, abr. and repr. in *The Honest to God Debate.*

17. *Ibid.,* p. 231.

18. R. J. Campbell, *The New Theology* (New York: Macmillan, 1907); Charles Gore, *The New Theology and the Old Religion* (New York: Dutton, 1907), a critical review, and *The Holy Spirit and the Church* (London: Murray, 1924), Chap. X. See also A. M. Ramsey, *An Era of Anglican Theology* (New York: Scribner, 1960), Chaps. 5 and 6.

19. *Nature, Man, and God* (London: Macmillan, 1935), esp. Chaps. 10, 11, 12.

20. *The Honest to God Debate,* p. 260.

21. *Honest to God,* p. 34.

22. E.g., Daniel Jenkins in *The Honest to God Debate,* pp. 207 f.

23. *Honest to God,* p. 10.

24. *The Honest to God Debate,* p. 262.

25. For critical evaluations of *Soundings* (New York: Cambridge University Press, 1962), see *Theology,* Nov., 1962; E. L. Mascall, *Up and Down in Adria* (London: Faith, 1963); *Four Anchors from the Stern,* ed. by Alan Richardson; and Roger Lloyd, *The Ferment in the Church,* Chap. 1. Dr. Mascall's reply is the subject of a critical essay by Ian Henderson in *Prism,* Jan., 1963.

26. *Soundings,* p. 162.

27. *Ibid.,* p. 172.

28. Quoted in *Honest to God,* p. 9.

29. *Ibid.,* p. 18.

30. D. M. MacKinnon, H. E. Root, H. W. Montefiore, and J. Burnaby, *God, Sex, and War* (Philadelphia: Westminster, 1965).

31. Paul Van Buren, *The Secular Meaning of the Gospel* (New York: Macmillan, 1963), p. 103.

32. Quoted in *The Honest to God Debate,* pp. 246 f.

33. See A. M. Ramsey, *An Era of Anglican Theology,* Chap. 6.

34. Specifically, the word as I am using it has nothing to do with its use in the presidential election in the United States in 1964!

35. Alec R. Vidler, *Essays in Liberality* (London: SCM, 1957), pp. 21 f. and *passim.*

Chapter 8: Natural Theology: The Sick Man of Europe

1. J. A. T. Robinson, *The New Reformation?* (Philadelphia: Westminster, 1965), pp. 106-122.

2. Dietrich Bonhoeffer, *Prisoner for God: Letters and Papers from Prison* (New York: Macmillan, 1954), pp. 145 ff.

3. Paul Van Buren, *The Secular Meaning of the Gospel* (New York: Macmillan, 1963), p. 103.

4. Howard E. Root in *Soundings,* ed. by Alec R. Vidler (New York: Cambridge University Press, 1962), p. 6. For criticism of Mr. Root's essay, see E. L. Mascall, *Up and Down in Adria* (London: Faith, 1963), pp. 16 ff.

5. *The Honest to God Debate,* ed. by David L. Edwards (Philadelphia: Westminster, 1963), p. 20.

6. *Ibid.*

7. Natural theology is "that body of knowledge about God which may be obtained by human reason alone without the aid of revelation." *The Oxford Dictionary of the Christian Church,* ed. by F. L. Cross (London: Oxford, 1957), p. 940.

8. See Temple's remarks quoted in the Introduction, *supra.*

9. "I conclude, then, that there is, after all, a sense in which we can properly inquire and even say, 'what it really means to say so and so.' For we can ask what is the real form of the fact recorded when this is concealed or disguised and not dully exhibited by the expression in question. And we can often succeed in stating this fact in a new form of words which does exhibit what the other failed to exhibit. And I am for the present inclined to believe that this is what philosophical analysis is, and that this is the sole and whole function of philosophy. . . . I would rather allot to philosophy a sublimer task than the detection of the sources in linguistic idioms of recurrent misconstructions and absurd theories. But that it is at least this I cannot feel any serious doubt." Gilbert Ryle, *Essays on Logic and Language,* 1st Ser., ed. by A. G. N. Flew (New York: Philosophical Library, 1951), p. 36, cited by H. E. Root in *Theology,* Oct., 1960, pp. 404 f.

10. Quoted by Howard E. Root, *op. cit.,* 405. Ayer modified his position somewhat in the Preface to the 2nd ed. of *Language, Truth and Logic.* For a critical evaluation of his views, see E. L. Mascall, *Words and Images* (London: Longmans, 1957), pp. 1-14.

11. See Alec R. Vidler, *20th Century Defenders of the Faith* (New York: Seabury, 1965), pp. 79-101.

12. *Natural Theology,* comprising "Nature and Grace" by Emil Brunner and the reply "No!" by Karl Barth, trans. by Peter Fraenkel (London: Bles, 1956).

13. Walter Lowrie, *A Short Life of Kierkegaard* (Princeton, N.J.: Princeton University Press, 1942), pp. 261 ff.

14. Søren Kierkegaard, *Philosophical Fragments* (Princeton, N.J.: Princeton University Press, 1944), and *Concluding Unscientific Postscript* (Princeton, N.J.: Princeton University Press, 1944).

15. For a criticism of Farrer's and Mascall's views, see Ronald W. Hepburn, *Christianity and Paradox* (New York: Humanities, 1956), Chaps. 9 and 10.

16. Alan Richardson, *Four Anchors from the Stern* (Naperville, Ill.: Allenson, 1963), pp. 8 ff.

17. See Chap. 3, *supra.*

18. For surveys of the changing attitude in philosophical circles, see Howard E. Root, "Some Features of Philosophical Theology in Britain: 1939-1960," *Theology,* Oct., 1960, pp. 401-408, and Basil Mitchell, ed.,

Faith and Logic (London: Allen & Unwin, 1957), particularly Mr. Mitchell's Introduction, pp. 1-8.

19. *New Essays in Philosophical Theology,* ed. by Antony Flew and Alasdair MacIntyre (London: Macmillan, 1955); *Faith and Logic,* ed. by Basil Mitchell; Ian T. Ramsey, *Religious Language* (Naperville, Ill.: Allenson, 1957); Stephen Toulmin, Ronald W. Hepburn, and Alasdair MacIntyre, *Metaphysical Beliefs* (London: SCM, 1958); Ronald W. Hepburn, *Christianity and Paradox;* Ian T. Ramsey, *Freedom and Immortality* (London: SCM, 1960); Michael B. Foster, *Mystery and Philosophy* (London: SCM, 1960); *Prospect for Metaphysics,* ed. by Ian T. Ramsey (London: Allen & Unwin, 1961); E. L. Mascall, *Theology and Images* (London: Mowbray, 1963).

20. *Soundings,* pp. 161 f.

21. *Ibid.,* p. 13.

22. *Ibid.,* p. 118.

23. Psalm 8; Psalm 19:1-6; Psalm 102:25-28; Psalm 103; Psalm 139: 1-16; Job, Chap. 38 through Chap. 42:6; Isaiah 6:1-12; Isaiah 10:1-19; Jeremiah 1; Amos, Chaps. 6 and 7. These and innumerable passages express the *religious* faith that God is the creator and preserver of this world, that God's originating and sustaining creativity reflects his purpose, and that God's presence and purpose are to be discerned in the moral decisions that confront individuals and social groups day by day.

24. See his *Monologium* and *Prologium* (LaSalle, Ill.: Open Court, 1910).

25. Seen note 9, *supra.*

26. Bultmann's essay and the debate it provoked may be followed in *Kerygma and Myth,* ed. by Hans Werner Bartsch and trans. by Reginald H. Fuller (London: SPCK, Vol. 1, 1953, Vol. 2, 1962).

27. For English reactions to the debate, see Austin Farrer's essay in *Kerygma and Myth,* Vol. 1, pp. 212 ff; Ian Henderson, *Myth in the New Testament* (London: SCM, 1952); and A. M. Ramsey, *Durham Essays and Addresses* (London: SPCK, 1956), pp. 29 ff. Reginald H. Fuller, *The New Testament in Current Study* (London: SCM, 1963), is perhaps the most balanced and complete evaluation in English.

28. *The Secular Meaning of the Gospel;* see particularly the conclusion, pp. 193 ff.

29. See, e.g., Ronald W. Hepburn's essay in *Objections to Humanism* (London: Constable, 1964).

30. J. A. T. Robinson's reply to Alasdair MacIntyre in *The Honest to God Debate,* pp. 228 ff., and Myron B. Bloy, Jr., *The Crisis of Cultural*

Change (New York: Seabury, 1965), together with the various writings of Gibson Winter.

31. Paul Tillich, *Systematic Theology* (Chicago: University of Chicago Press, Vol. 1, 1951; Vol. 2, 1957; Vol. 3, 1963). *The Shaking of the Foundations* (1952), *The New Being* (1955), and *The Eternal Now* (1963) are collections of sermons (all: New York: Scribner). *The New Being* (New Haven, Conn.: Yale University Press, 1952), *Love, Power, and Justice* (London: Oxford, 1954), and *Biblical Religion and the Search for Ultimate Reality* (Chicago: University of Chicago Press, 1955) are series of lectures which supplement the *Systematic Theology* at important points, as does *Dynamics of Faith* (New York: Harper & Row, 1957). Collections of essays include *The Protestant Era* (Chicago: University of Chicago Press, 1948) and *Theology of Culture* (London: Oxford, 1959).

32. J. Heywood Thomas, *Paul Tillich: An Appraisal* (London: SCM, 1963), and Ninian Smart, "The Intellectual Crisis of British Christianity," *Theology,* Jan., 1965, pp. 31 ff.

33. See *Honest to God* (Philadelphia: Westminster, 1963), p. 56.

34. Paul Tillich, *Systematic Theology,* Vol, 2, p. 152.

35. *Cf.* Chap. 3.

36. *Cf.* Tillich's discussion of his method of correlation in the *Systematic Theology,* Vol. 1, pp. 6 ff., and the Introduction to Vol. 2.

37. *Religious Language,* Chaps. 3 and 4. The same methods are utilized in Ramsey's *On Being Sure in Religion* (New York: Oxford, 1963) and *Religion and Science: Conflict and Synthesis* (London: SPCK, 1964).

38. Alan Richardson, *History, Sacred and Profane* (Philadelphia: Westminster, 1964), and T. A. Roberts, *History and Christian Apologetic* (London: SPCK, 1960).

39. In *Kerygma and Myth,* Vol. 1, pp. 212 ff. (New York: Harper Torchbook ed., 1961).

40. Writing of liberal Protestantism in the United States in 1935, Reinhold Niebuhr observed: "The culture of modernity was the artifact of modern civilization, product of its unique and characteristic conditions, and it is therefore not surprising that its minarets of the spirit should fall when the material foundations of its civilization begin to crumble. Its optimism had no more solid foundation than the expansive mood of the era of triumphant capitalism and naturally gives way to confusion and despair when the material conditions of life are seriously altered. Therefore the lights of its towers are extinguished at the very moment when light is needed to survey the havoc wrought in the city and the plan of rebuilding." *An Interpretation of Christian Ethics* (New York: Harper & Row, 1935).

41. In "Burnt Norton," *Four Quartets* (New York: Harcourt, Brace & World, 1943).

42. *Cf. Soundings,* pp. 18 f.

43. William G. Pollard, *Chance and Providence* (New York: Scribner, 1958), and *Physicist and Christian* (New York: Seabury, 1961), together with John S. Habgood, *Truths in Tension* (New York: Holt, Rinehart & Winston, 1965), are illustrative of this kind of interest.

Chapter 9: Morality in a Post-Christian Society

1. "Christian ethics has for the most part concerned itself with general principles and moral theology with their application to specific cases. . . . The two belong together and should be two parts of one study dealing with Christian principles of behavior and their application—there is no basic opposition between them." Herbert Waddams, *A New Introduction to Moral Theology* (New York: Seabury, 1965), p. 24.

2. Ronald Preston, "Christian Ethics and Moral Theology, 1939-60," *Theology,* Jan., 1961, pp. 6 f. The article appears in two parts, the second being found in *Theology,* Feb., 1961, pp. 46 ff., and contains an admirable annotated bibliography of the important literature in English from 1939 to 1960. The journal *Christendom* first appeared in Mar., 1931, and ceased publication in 1950. Its chief contributors came to be referred to as the Christendom group. For mention of their chief works, together with criticisms of them, see Ronald Preston, *op. cit.,* pp. 6 ff., and D. L. Munby, "The Importance of Technical Competence," *Essays in Anglican Self-Criticism* (London: SCM, 1958), pp. 45-58, also *Theology,* Mar., 1961, p. 110.

3. Herbert Waddams, *op. cit.,* pp. 11 ff.

4. J. S. Bezzant in *Theology,* Mar., 1961, p. 99.

5. *Honest to God* (Philadelphia: Westminster, 1963), p. 105.

6. The phrase "the new morality" was used on Feb. 2, 1956, by the Supreme Sacred Congregation of the Holy Office to describe the "existential," or "situational," ethics condemned by Pope Pius XII in an allocution on Apr. 18, 1952. See *Acta Apostolicae Sedis,* 44 (1952), pp. 413-419. The phrase gained prominence in English circles when used as the heading for Chap. 6 of *Honest to God.*

7. J. A. T. Robinson, *Christian Morals Today* (Philadelphia: Westminster, 1964), pp. 8 ff. Also Lindsay Dewar, *Moral Theology in the Modern World* (London: Mowbray, 1964), Chap. 4, esp. pp. 54 f.

8. For the contributions of Maurice, Gore, Temple, and others, see M. B. Reckitt, *Maurice to Temple* (London: Faber & Faber, 1947). On Gore, *cf.* G. L. Prestige, *The Soul of a Prophet* (London: SPCK, 1948), and James Carpenter, *Gore* (London: Faith, 1960), Chap. 9. On Temple, see Joseph Fletcher, *William Temple* (New York: Seabury, 1963), esp. Part III, and Robert Craig, *Social Concern in the Thought of William Temple* (Naperville, Ill.: Allenson, 1963), together with John D. Carmichael and

Harold S. Goodwin, *William Temple's Political Legacy* (London: Mowbray, 1963).

9. D. L. Munby, *op. cit.,* p. 49; Herbert Waddams, *op. cit.,* p. 40.

10. William Temple, *Christianity and the Social Order* (London: Penguin, 1942), esp. Chaps. 4 and 5.

11. Joseph Fletcher, *Morals and Medicine* (Princeton, N.J.: Princeton University Press, 1954); Thomas Wood, *Some Moral Problems* (London: SPCK, 1961); D. M. MacKinnon, H. E. Root, H. W. Montefiore, and John Burnaby, *God, Sex, and War* (Philadelphia: Westminster, 1965).

12. See the editorial in *Theology,* Mar., 1965, pp. 121-123. Pamphlets similar to the ones referred to have been produced by the British Council of Churches and the National Council of Churches in the U.S.A. on a wide range of topics.

13. Alec R. Vider, *Christ's Strange Work* (London: SCM, 1963 ed.), pp. 107 ff.

14. Alec R. Vidler, *op. cit.,* Chaps. 8, 9. See also Alden D. Kelley, *Christianity and Political Responsibility* (Philadelphia: Westminster, 1961). Of the various books written with Z in mind, the most helpful are C. S. Lewis, *Christian Behavior* (New York: Macmillan, 1943); James A Pike, *Doing the Truth* (Garden City, N.Y.: Doubleday, 1955); and Stephen F. Bayne, *Christian Living* (New York: Seabury, 1957).

15. Alec R. Vidler, *op. cit.,* p. 118.

16. Kenneth E. Kirk's major works on moral theology include *Some Principles of Moral Theology* (London: Longmans, 1920), *Ignorance, Faith, and Conformity* (London: Longmans, 1925), *Conscience and Its Problems* (London: Longmans, 1927), *The Vision of God* (London: Longmans, 1931), and *Marriage and Divorce* (London: Hodder & Stoughton, 1932 ed.). J. S. Bezzant has given a recent appraisal of Kirk's contribution in *Theology,* Mar., 1961, pp. 96-99.

17. Ronald Preston, summarizing criticisms made in 1939 by M. B. Stewart, *Theology,* Jan., 1961, p. 4.

18. R. C. Mortimer, *Elements of Moral Theology* (London: Black, 1953 ed.); Lindsay Dewar and Cyril Hudson, *Christian Morals* (London: Hodder & Stoughton, 1945); Lindsay Dewar, *A Short Introduction to Moral Theology* (London: Mowbray, 1956), together with his *Moral Theology in the Modern World.*

19. Kenneth E. Kirk, *The Study of Theology* (London: Hodder & Stoughton, 1939), p. 383, and Joseph Fletcher, "The New Look in Christian Ethics," *Harvard Divinity Bulletin,* Oct., 1959, p. 14.

20. Kenneth E. Kirk, *Some Principles of Moral Theology,* Preface and Chap. 2. *Cf.* H. R. MacAdoo, *The Structure of Caroline Moral Theology*

(London: Longmans, 1949), and Thomas Wood, *English Casuistical Divinity* (London: SPCK, 1952), which substantiate Kirk's point concerning the differences in emphasis between Roman Catholic and Anglican moral theology on the historical side.

21. Ed. by Alec R. Vidler (London: SPCK, 1964). The essays initially appeared in *Theology*, Nov., 1961-Aug., 1963.

22. Herbert Waddams, *Life and Fire of Love* (London: SPCK, 1964). In linking moral and ascetical theology, Canon Waddams follows the lead of Kenneth E. Kirk.

23. *Honest to God*, Chap. 5.

24. Joseph Fletcher, *op. cit.*, p. 17.

25. *Ibid.*, p. 10.

26. Paul Tillich, *Theology of Culture* (New York: Oxford, 1959), pp. 133-146.

27. J. A. T. Robinson, *Christian Morals Today*, p. 10.

28. H. A. Williams in *Soundings,* ed. by Alec R. Vidler (New York: Cambridge University Press, 1962), pp. 80 ff., and *Objections to Christian Belief,* ed. by Alec R. Vidler (Philadelphia: Lippincott, 1964), pp. 35 ff.

29. D. A. Rhymes, *No New Morality* (New York: Bobbs-Merrill, 1964).

30. Perhaps the clearest statement of the place of law in the Christian life is to be found in Alec R. Vidler, *Christ's Strange Work.* See also H. Oppenheimer, *Law and Love* (London: Faith, 1962), and G. F. Thomas, *Christian Ethics and Moral Philosophy* (New York: Scribner, 1955), pp. 105-141.

31. There has been good work done on the doctrine of man in recent years by Anglican writers such as G. F. Thomas, *op. cit.,* pp. 145-218; Edmond Cherbonnier, *Hardness of Heart* (Garden City, N.Y.: Doubleday, 1955); E. L. Mascall, *The Importance of Being Human* (New York: Columbia University Press, 1958); Stephen Neill, *A Genuinely Human Existence* (Garden City, N.Y.: Doubleday, 1959); and W. Norman Pittenger, *The Christian Understanding of Human Nature* (Philadelphia: Westminster, 1964). It does not seem to have affected the 1963-64 discussion in England, however.

32. Harry C. Meserve, "The New Morality," *Journal of Religion and Health*, Jan., 1964, pp. 115-118.

Index